Getting Physical

GETTING PHYSICAL

How to Stick with Your
Exercise Program

Art Turock

Doubleday
New York
1988

Library of Congress Cataloging in Publication Data

Turock, Art, 1950–
  Getting physical.

  1. Exercise.   2. Motivation (Psychology)   I. Title.
RA781.T87   1988   613.7'1   87-13436
ISBN 0-385-24297-2

ACKNOWLEDGEMENTS

Many thanks to:

- My father, Julius Turock, for providing the inspiration to write this book.
- Dr. Elizabeth Neeld, my writing coach, who has contributed to my development as a writer.
- Dr. Kenneth Cooper, who is a role model of a man who has influenced the physical fitness of millions of people.
- Ken Blanchard, co-author of *The One Minute Manager,* who inspired me to try to write a book that makes a difference.
- Kyle Winn and Werner Erhard, who helped me realize the incredible power of making commitments to big results.
- The thousands of on-again, off-again exercisers who've shared their struggles with me.

CONTENTS

Getting
Physical

The Missing Ingredient— Motivation

"What do you do for a living?" asked the man sitting next to me on the plane.

"I help people to motivate themselves to stick with exercise," I replied.

"Motivation . . . now that's what I need."

"What motivates you to exercise?"

"When I look in a mirror and notice my belly getting fatter."

"How often do you exercise?"

"Twice a month I use the rowing machine."

"So your fitness program is on hold while you're waiting to get fatter. Your body has to get in worse condition, so you'll feel motivated to get in shape."

Does starting a regular exercise program sound like a great idea until you discover the only available time is six o'clock in the morning? Is the exercise bike you got for Christmas collecting dust because you'd rather read a book or watch TV after a hard day's work? Do you decline invitations to aerobics classes because you feel too fat in a T-shirt and shorts? Maybe your feelings about exercise are captured by W.C. Fields who said, "Every time I get the urge to exercise, I lie down and wait until it passes."

Perhaps starting an exercise program is easy but the real problem is sticking with it. Has your pattern been to get off to a blistering start, only to have hectic work schedules, relationship hassles, or travel disrupt your routine? Maybe a movie star's exercise videotape inspired you. After months of working out faithfully, you still don't look trim and beautiful. Your favorite celebrity now sounds like a drill sergeant. Time again to call it quits. Although you see value in exercise and have a workout routine, doing it regularly is a struggle.

Maybe you've reached a plateau in your fitness program. You've been doing the same routine for months, but higher level fitness is your goal. You've thought about intensifying your program and even consulted with fitness professionals. Unfortunately, the desire to push yourself dies as you enter the gym. You see value in doing a more challenging program, but there is still something missing.

What's missing is motivation. Not motivation as a hype, but motivation that lasts forever. *Getting Physical* is the exercise book for people who value being physically fit but have difficulty putting together a fit lifestyle. It starts a step back from assuming you already have the proper motivation. This is the fitness book you've been waiting for—the one that teaches you how to motivate yourself to stick with regular exercise, not for a few weeks but for the rest of your life.

It took triple coronary bypass surgery to wake me up to the need for a way to build exercise motivation. My father's operation in February 1983 alerted me to the gap between knowledge and action. Knowing the heart disease risk factors had made no difference for my father. He had continued to smoke, eat high cholesterol foods, and carry excess weight, and had rarely exercised. He had rationalized that changing habits was inconvenient, and besides, there were better things to do. When I heard that he needed the operation, I realized that my father was like millions of Americans working hard to get ahead and achieve "the good life" at any cost. All too often, the cost is their health.

My father has recovered from surgery and now walks twenty to thirty minutes every day. But waiting until the threat of death creates a motivation to exercise is not wise. As a fitness motivator, my challenge is to help people see the urgency of adopting a fitness program, not only as a health measure but to support the overall quality of life.

Getting hooked on exercise fifteen years ago changed my life. I grew up in a body I hated. Throughout high school, I considered myself skinny and unattractive. I remember my friend's brother putting a thumb and finger around my bicep when I was a freshman and almost being able to touch the fingertips.

My transformation began in college when I was introduced to weight lifting. After several months of training, my friends started to ask, "Where'd you get the new body?" My self-confidence soared.

While many people have conversion experiences through religion, personal growth workshops, or crises, my early breakthroughs came from rigorous workouts. Sustaining a regular exercise program has been a training ground for valuable habits such as goal-setting, self-discipline, persistence, and confronting difficulty. I have now been weight lifting and running for nearly eighteen years.

My fitness hobby has now become part of my life's work. I develop corporate fitness programs, coach individual executives, and lead seminars on motivation and habit change. My corporate clients have included RCA, Weyerhaeuser, Corona Clipper, the Seattle Police Department, and Blanchard Training and Development. I have provided training for the Association of Physical Fitness Centers and the

National Employee Services and Recreation Association. Research with hundreds of individuals indicates these methods achieve some of the highest rates of regular exercise in the fitness field.

In my corporate fitness programs, approximately seven out of ten participants have maintained a regular exercise program (a minimum of three workouts of at least thirty minutes per week) six to twelve months after start-up. This is well above the norm, in which 50 percent typically drop out after six months. In one group of managers at a manufacturing company in California, only one person dropped out of my program over an entire year. Only one third of this group was exercising regularly before this program.

The participants in my corporate programs had been primarily on-again, off-again exercisers. For many participants, high school graduation marked their last extended period of consistent exercise. They had made lots of short-lived attempts to lose weight and stay in shape. They knew the benefits of exercise but couldn't adjust their lifestyles to include regular workouts. Jobs and families had to come first, and health would have to suffer if time ran short. The trade-off was not satisfying. All along, they really wanted to have it all—career, family, and health. The motivational strategies in this book have worked for people of all ages and occupations who used every excuse on record for not exercising. If my clients can be successful, you can, too.

A question I'm often asked is, "Can someone who hasn't been motivated to exercise *learn* how to stick with it?" It's a great question because studies show that exercise is a difficult habit to develop. A 1985 Louis Harris Poll in *USA Today* reported that only 34 percent of adults say they "exercise strenuously" three or more times a week; 25 percent do so one or two times a week. In a review of exercise compliance studies, William J. Stone concluded that within six months, approximately 50 percent of those joining a fitness program will drop out. Some fitness programs have had a drop-out rate as high as 60 to 80 percent within one to two years. Do these kinds of statistics prove people lack motivation?

The statistics are misleading. Trash the statistics. *Beneath all the excuses given for not exercising is one basic truth—people want their bodies to work for them.* People are motivated to have the health and fitness that support a rich and fulfilling life.

What stops most people is their sense of the difficulties involved in sticking with a regular exercise program. But the difficulties are overrated. Notice that after people become steady exercisers, they look back on the old excuses and realize it wasn't so difficult to change.

I don't have to add motivation. I have to strip away the inflated sense of difficulty in establishing the exercise habit. I have to help people see how regular exercise is essential to creating the healthy, high-performance lifestyle they already desire.

The purpose of this book is to teach you the motivational secrets practiced by regular and high-performance exercisers. Consistent exercisers can appear to be a special breed of people blessed with a natural drive to be physically active. It seems as though push-ups, sit-ups, and jumping jacks are as routine as breathing for them. But what has become routine for regular exercisers is a style of thinking that supports sticking with their fitness programs. They naturally focus on the benefits of exercise and dismiss weak excuses for missing workouts. They automatically talk themselves into exercising while inconsistent exercisers talk themselves out of doing it. The bottom line is that regular exercisers think differently from infrequent exercisers.

Fortunately, the self-motivation skills of regular exercisers can be learned. The first step is to uncover subtle motivational traps that take over at moments when you're choosing whether to perform an exercise workout or to skip it. Right now, you don't recognize them as traps. They appear to be legitimate reasons for not exercising. They make it look as if real circumstances are keeping you from getting in shape.

You will soon come to recognize the motivational traps for what they really are—self-limiting patterns of thinking. By identifying these traps during real-life exercise opportunities, you will start to reprogram your thinking in ways that encourage exercise. Gradually, you will develop the new habit of noticing the value, not the difficulty of exercising. This shift in thinking will cause you to more easily choose to exercise instead of looking for reasons to stay inactive.

It will be apparent that self-motivation is not some innate capacity possessed by a select group of regular exercisers. Self-motivation requires mental skills. Any kind of skill development, physical or mental, requires practice. Just as practice improves a golf swing, practice develops self-motivation skills. Throughout this book are "Motivation Training Sessions" for building and refining your self-motivation skills. You will be guided step-by-step through the process of making and sustaining a fitness commitment. The Motivation Training Sessions are simple, time-efficient steps to integrate exercise into your life.

This book isn't only for on-again, off-again exercisers. It may help regular exercisers to gain an extra motivational edge. While exercising consistently is no longer an issue, regular exercisers may have difficulty intensifying their workouts. They think about more challenging fitness goals but never adjust their exercise programs. Motivational traps that plague sporadic exercisers are the same ones that stop regular exercisers from pursuing higher level fitness. Here's the opportunity to go beyond an exercise plateau.

Your capacity for self-motivation is about to be released.

- You can make exercise a permanent habit instead of a seasonal fling after every New Year's and before each swimsuit season.

- You can stay motivated even when demands at work and at home are not conducive to an exercise routine —not just exercising during good weeks but even when your busy schedule gets crazy.

- You can get in shape and maintain good condition without decreasing productivity at work or weakening important relationships and family ties.

- You can become a regular exerciser without much athletic background or success in earlier exercise programs.

- You can make exercise enjoyable and not so boring.

- Your exercise program can become easy and natural without lots of struggle with self-discipline.

2

The Difference Between Regular Exercisers and Everybody Else

A workshop participant said, "Art, I'm a procrastinator. What should I do about it?"

I replied, *"Do something!"*

(I thought to myself, "This guy probably thinks he was born with a deficiency of willpower genes.")

How important is your health? Are you thinking, "What is this, a trick question?" You will probably answer, "Health is my number one priority. Without good health, nothing else matters." But the main reason people give for not exercising is "interference from other priorities."

This isn't to say people are hypocrites. We value being physically fit but many of us haven't integrated exercise into our lives. Despite good intentions, unfavorable circumstances stop us. We remain on the verge of adopting a fit lifestyle.

We all know people who exercise consistently, sometimes more than five hours a week. Where do they find the time and energy? How do they stay motivated week after week?

Regular exercisers seem to be different from everybody else. They seem to be born with the drive to run, jump, sweat, and to move their bodies. Instead of being a chore for them, exercise is fun and invigorating.

Before the fitness movement, regular exercisers were considered exceptional, maybe even weird. They were called health nuts, fitness fanatics, and exercise junkies.

Times have changed. Your previously inactive friends are joining health clubs, buying exercise bikes, entering 10K runs, and even talking about personal records. How did they make this transformation from slugs to regular exercisers?

The difference between infrequent and regular exercisers isn't as great as it may seem. It is easy to make exercise a habit.

WE'RE GREAT STARTERS BUT ROTTEN COMPLETERS

If we could go to an auction and buy good health, stress relief, an eye-catching physique, or vibrant energy, the bids would be high. We value the benefits of regular exercise. Even after repeated lay-offs, many of us keep starting up exercise programs.

We tend to be great starters but rotten completers. "Wake-up events" get us back to exercise: We get orders from a doctor. We notice cellulite on the thighs. We run short of breath when playing with our children. We become enamored of the new office hunk whose favorite pastime is racquetball.

The inspired start doesn't last. If circumstances change, exercise drops out of the routine. However, fitness isn't a short-term project. After just one month of inactivity, muscles atrophy, energy drops, and heart and lung capacity diminish. Fitness endures only with regular exercise.

Exercise poses a basic dilemma. We want our bodies to be fit and healthy. At the same time, we want to avoid the effort required to stay in shape. We are attracted to the benefits exercise offers and discouraged by the apparent difficulty of achieving lasting results.

If your exercise pattern is filled with starts and stops, you have fallen into the habit of noticing difficulties in maintaining an exercise program. Where will extra time come from in your hectic schedule? Where can you find a less crowded pool so you can swim laps during lunch hour? How will you get the support of family members who want you at home during your preferred workout times? How can you maintain a fixed workout schedule when your job involves out-of-town travel, entertaining clients, and extra paperwork at night? If your body has gotten far out of shape, is it worth all the effort to regain lost strength and stamina?

Even when you're exercising regularly, the habit of noticing difficulties persists. What if your trimmer, more attractive body stirs up jealousy or envy in your spouse or a close friend? If your desired results don't come fast enough, will you get disillusioned and quit, wasting all the effort you have expended? Does getting in shape now force you to exercise for the rest of your life to keep in good condition? It seems so formidable!

There is no denying these circumstances exist. But circumstances are only circumstances. Seeing them as permanent barriers to exercise is your own doing.

Lack of time does not prevent regular exercise. Feeling too tired, being under stress, or finding exercise boring are not the causes of sporadic exercise.

The knowledge of one fact can be a source of breakthroughs—*your difficulties in sticking with exercise are all made up. Calling a circumstance a difficulty causes sporadic exercise.* Right now, you may be thinking, "Now wait a minute. You don't know my circumstances. My difficulties are real." The difficulties *look* real to you. You've fallen into the habit of accepting these circumstances as true barriers to exercise.

Take a look at any time in your life when you successfully completed a project you thought was impossible. For instance, you faced an unreasonable deadline at work. Your boss underestimated the time required. The computer had been acting up all day. It was Friday afternoon and your co-workers were eagerly awaiting the weekend. Last-minute work was bound to be met with resistance.

The circumstances looked overwhelming for completing the assignment, yet somehow you finished on time. Afterwards, you may have had thoughts like, "That wasn't as difficult as I'd imagined" or "It was a real effort but it wasn't impossible." The difficulty had all been in your mind.

How did you finish off this rush assignment? You might respond, "I had no choice. I've got to keep my job to put food on the table." But do you have a choice when it comes to your health? Isn't being healthy just as important to your survival as making money to afford life's essentials?

It's all a matter of perception. When the results of an activity are perceived as valuable, potential difficulties are dismissed. We just do what needs to get done.

The same principle applies to exercise. So long as perceived difficulty exceeds perceived value, exercise will be inconsistent. When you value fitness enough, there are no difficulties that can't be overcome.

The good news is that perceptions of difficulty and value are your own creations. At any moment, you carry on a dialogue with yourself about whether the immediate conditions are "right" for exercise. How you perceive the circumstances, not the circumstances themselves, determine your actions. For instance, there may be times when the fifteen-minute drive to the gym seems too inconvenient, yet a few weeks before the distance was unimportant. You just did it. Going on a vacation can be perceived either as a time for total rest or as free time to intensify an exercise program.

Notice the flexibility of perceptions. Our perceptions of value and difficulty are not "the way things are." They can always be adjusted to support your desire to get regular exercise.

THE MAKE-OR-BREAK FACTOR

Only one make-or-break factor separates regular exercisers from everybody else. In its absence, exercise is a struggle and often doesn't get done. In its presence, all difficulties lose their power. Supposedly valid reasons for not exercising seem to vanish.

> *The key to success with exercise is commitment. If you've been irregular with exercise, the only thing stopping you is lack of commitment.*

What is the difference between "being committed" and merely "being interested" in fitness? The difference becomes clear by looking at the outcomes.

Infrequent exercisers are interested in the benefits of exercise but are not committed to being physically fit. Although the benefits seem attractive, infrequent exercisers often sidetrack themselves by perceiving inconvenience and discomfort when they consider exercising. Instead of exercising, they think and talk about becoming fit. "I want to get back in shape but . . ." "I know I should get more exercise but . . ." "I've been planning on exercising this week but . . ." The outcome of being merely interested is having good reasons for not exercising regularly.

What reasons do you give for falling short of your exercise goals? Whatever the reasons, you probably feel like you're doing your best under difficult circumstances. However, what feels like your best shot is a self-deception. You're really doing what's realistic, manageable, reasonable, comfortable, and easy. It seems too difficult to make the extra effort. Ultimately, you settle for being less fit than you'd like to be.

The trap is giving up responsibility for your own fitness and leaving it up to the circumstances. No wonder your exercise program is inconsistent. Sometimes circumstances are conducive to exercise and sometimes they are not. Thinking "if only circumstances would change" puts you in a holding pattern. Wishing and hoping for a change of circumstances doesn't make any difference, except that you get more out of shape. *Exercising "if circumstances permit" simply doesn't work.*

Commitment is very different from interest. The outcome of commitment is results. Committed people take action to get desired results *no matter what* difficulty is present. A shift in perception occurs. The perceived value of being fit is now so great that the difficulties of exercising regularly seem less significant. Exercise becomes worth the extra effort.

Commitment involves deciding that "this exercise program will be done" and then doing it. No reasons, just results.

Here is what commitment looks like:

- When a workout is missed, it is immediately rescheduled. The excuse "it's okay to miss one every once in a while" isn't tolerated.

- When a string of workouts is missed, regular sessions resume promptly. Waiting for the "slump" to pass and for enthusiasm to return is unacceptable.

- During an unusually busy period, workouts may be scaled down slightly. However, a "bad week" is not a sufficient excuse for a layoff.

- Despite thinking of reasons for not exercising, committed exercisers go ahead and do it anyway. The reasons don't matter, results do.

- Plans for intensifying an exercise program are acted on. Committed exercisers don't repeat the same program month after month because it is comfortable, at the expense of their desired fitness results.

The best signs of commitment are the choices we make in the face of difficulty. Only two choices are available. Accept reasons for not exercising or do what it takes to get results. At the moment of truth, it all boils down to one question: What's it going to be, reasons or results?

	Outcome	Perceived Difficulty	Basis for Action
Interest	Reasons	> Perceived Value	If Circumstances Permit
Commitment	Results	Perceived Value > Perceived Difficulty	No Matter What

Interested people are in the habit of tolerating reasons for missing or putting off exercise. They are committed to avoiding difficulty. This explains why someone can value the benefits of exercise, have good intentions, know what to do, yet not follow through consistently.

Committed people take difficulties in stride and overcome them. Taking action "no matter what" is very different from acting only "if circumstances permit."

At first glance, the thought of doing something "no matter what" may seem unreasonable. After all, you don't want to be branded a fitness fanatic. Actually, we do very little that is considered difficult unless we feel "no matter what" about the results. Look at other areas of your life. Think about all the hassles of getting to work on time that you master every morning. What about going out of your way to keep promises to your family or to business customers? What about paying your mortgage every month? The "no matter what" posture isn't so rare.

Getting Physical is designed to cause a shift from interest to full-fledged commitment.

GROUND RULES FOR SUCCESS

If you were to ask me right now, "Will this book work for me?" I would answer, "It depends on you." The program has worked for hundreds of my seminar participants and clients. It worked because they were willing to follow conscientiously four ground rules. You'll want to follow them too.

1. Forget your past track record.

The question "Will it work?" comes from reflecting on your past history with exercise. Your pattern has been to check out exercise programs to find one you can stick with. However, the real problem isn't finding the right program. Any exercise program will be done consistently when you're committed to it.

Give yourself a fresh start. Concentrate on creating a commitment to a physically fit lifestyle.

2. Put your learnings into action.

Don't expect to be motivated by magic words. Words on a page don't provide lasting motivation.

Enduring results come from applying specific skills and strategies of self-motivation. You will be learning how to sustain a lifelong commitment to being physically fit.

The best way to learn any new skill is through plenty of practice. Over a lifetime, there will be no shortage of occasions to practice it. Every time you consider exercising, you have a practice opportunity. You will either succumb to old excuses or follow through with your planned workout. Very soon, the deliberate effort to practice self-motivation will become second nature. The excuses will seem ridiculous and you'll just go and exercise.

3. Be willing to take an honest look at how you (and not life's circumstances) stop yourself from exercising regularly.

Don't complain about unfavorable circumstances and wait for them to change. But don't beat yourself up for making excuses either. Feeling guilty seems to give you permission to keep missing workouts.

Instead, examine your role in causing an exercise slump. Ask yourself: How am I making exercise a struggle? What reasons am I creating and accepting for giving up on my exercise program? What can I do right now to pull out of this slump?

4. Actively participate in this book.

Don't read this as if it were a romance novel. Reading for entertainment will lead to short-lived motivation. Instead, focus on developing specific self-motivation skills. Highlight key points, record insights on page margins or a sheet of paper, write answers to questions in the motivation training sessions.

Read this book as if it were the final piece of motivation you'll ever need to make exercise a lifelong habit. With that kind of commitment, it will be.

3

No One Exercises on Impulse

> "Everybody wants to be on a champion-
> ship team, but nobody wants to come to
> practice."
>
> —Bobby Knight,
> Basketball Coach, Indiana
> University; 1984 U.S. Olympic
> Team

In a 1985 survey of New Year's resolutions, *U.S.A. Today* reported that 75% of women and 65% of men who made resolutions said that they wanted to get more exercise. However, the success rate for exercise resolutions is poor.

Here's an example of what often happens. Today is the day Jane is supposed to start her New Year's resolution to lose a few pounds and get back in shape. It has been a rough day at work. She feels exhausted. Her in-basket is filled with assignments. Of course, it would be inexcusable to go and exercise until everything is completed (even though the work isn't due for several days).

Rain flows down the office window. Jogging in that downpour would be ridiculous. Driving to the YWCA would mean missing her favorite TV show. Besides, Jane's been thinking all day long, "Why pressure myself by trying to squeeze in exercise today? I stuck with my diet and avoided the chocolate cake at lunch. So what if I miss one exercise session! I'll make up for it with an extra-long run tomorrow."

Sounds like a very reasonable decision, right? Actually Jane is sabotaging her own exercise program. Without her commitment, reasons for not exercising are neverending. Gradually, the New Year's resolution is forgotten. Wait until next year.

No one exercises on impulse. Waiting for moments when exercising is convenient and you feel inspired doesn't work. These ideal moments are too infrequent to keep you in shape.

It's always going to be easier to remain inactive. Exercise involves taking extra time and making extra effort.

The purpose of this chapter is to take the mystery out of the process of self-motivation. You are your own worst enemy when it comes to sticking with exercise. At the same time, you are also your own best motivator. The difference boils down to commitment.

TWO MYTHS ABOUT MOTIVATION

Irregular exercisers often say they aren't motivated enough. They believe regular exercisers have a special inner strength. Believing that motivation is a matter of "you have it or you don't" is a mistake. Let's dispense with two popular myths about motivation.

Myth 1: You have to have the Right Stuff.

Have you ever heard someone say "I'm not the athletic type" or "I'm basically lazy" or "I'm not very self-disciplined"? These statements support the myth that we are born to be either active or inactive. Attributing lack of exercise to a genetic flaw makes behavior change impossible. You resign yourself to being one of those unfortunate people who failed to inherit proper motivation for exercise.

Fact: Motivation for exercise isn't genetically inherited.

It's a learned habit. Regular exercisers are in the habit of seeing the value of exercise and of diminishing its potential difficulties. Irregular exercisers do just the opposite. They exaggerate the difficulties to the point that the extra effort isn't worth it. It's a pattern of thinking that determines whether you leap into exercise or stay inactive. No one was born to be a couch potato.

Myth 2: If you wait, the magic will hit.

People often say they need to "get motivated," as if motivation depends on experiencing some powerful, life-changing event. They spend their lives waiting to fall under the magic spell of motivation. They say things like: "If only I could meet people who are enthusiastic about exercise!" and "I'm not overweight, so I don't need to exercise right now. When I get older and the weight starts to show, I'll be prepared to exercise."

Fact: No event can inspire you to exercise. Only the meaning you attach to events provides motivation.

What will it mean when you discover you can't fit into your favorite outfit? Will this be a signal to launch an exercise comeback or will it be evidence that you're too far out of shape to bother? What if you start a relationship with a devoted fitness buff? Will you see this relationship as a great opportunity for getting support for exercise or will you feel intimidated and pull out of the relationship?

Our own interpretations of events motivate us to action. At any moment, you can create perceptions that will either motivate or discourage exercise. It's not up to the circumstances any longer because your perceptions are your own choice.

CHOICE POINTS

Each time the option of exercising arises, we size up the benefits and difficulties and then decide whether or not to exercise. Regular exercisers appreciate the benefits so much that the difficulty involved seems insignificant. Infrequent exercisers don't see enough benefit to offset the apparent inconvenience and discomfort. This weighing of benefits and drawbacks is subtle. It often seems we don't have a real choice—as though the circumstances dictate whether or not we exercise.

Each time we consider exercising, a chain of events occurs. It works like this:

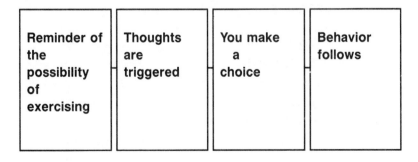

| Reminder of the possibility of exercising | Thoughts are triggered | You make a choice | Behavior follows |

For example, let's assume you want to lose fifteen pounds and improve your cardiovascular fitness. At the office, you tell your co-workers about this goal, never imagining anyone would care about your doing it. You hadn't counted on a close colleague being an aerobic dance enthusiast. She is delighted by your plans. "Why don't you join me at the noon aerobics class?" she says. "I know you'll love it."

Here is the chain of your thoughts:

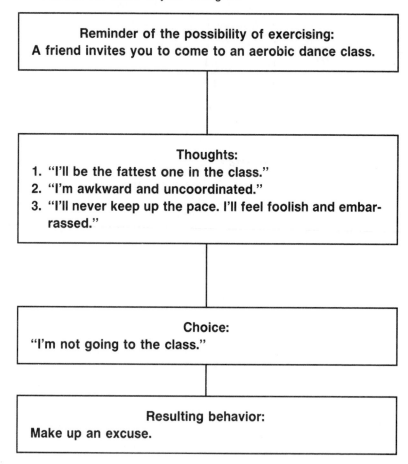

Reminder of the possibility of exercising:
A friend invites you to come to an aerobic dance class.

Thoughts:
1. **"I'll be the fattest one in the class."**
2. **"I'm awkward and uncoordinated."**
3. **"I'll never keep up the pace. I'll feel foolish and embarrassed."**

Choice:
"I'm not going to the class."

Resulting behavior:
Make up an excuse.

Declining the invitation pays off. You avoid feeling foolish and embarrassed. Notice that your own thoughts stopped you from saying yes.

If you've been irregular with exercise, you're caught in the habit of saying words to yourself that discourage physical activity. Your mind operates like a computer which is programmed from past experiences. This mental computer accesses files containing past associations with exercise. Files of irregular exercisers are filled with reminders of difficulty, discomfort, and lack of results. If they were numbered, the files of an irregular exerciser might look like this:

- File 101 reminds you of feeling out of breath and wanting to stop jogging.
- File 69 reminds you of all the false starts with prior exercise programs.
- File 24 warns you about the death of Jim Fixx while jogging.
- File 16 recalls that you are not a morning person and that early workouts go against human nature.

The files of regular exercisers are dominated by positive associations. The times when swimming sparked an immediate recovery from jet lag. The sense of accomplishment after setting a personal record or reaching a fitness goal. Stress relief from having a brisk game of racquetball after work.

Each time a reminder to exercise occurs, your mental computer automatically goes into action. If it is filled with negative associations of exercise, you're more likely to choose to stay inactive. It looks like you have no choice but to steer clear of exercise.

But you do have a choice. You don't have to give up control of your decisions to a pattern of fleeting thoughts. Regardless of your thoughts, you can choose to exercise.

You may be wondering, "How do I stick with exercise if my past experiences with it are ones of failure and struggle?" Follow the lead of regular exercisers. They think up excuses, too. The difference is that regular exercisers don't give any significance to reasons for not exercising. At the choice points, they might think: "Here I go again making up another reason for missing exercise. Just a fleeting thought that I'm in the habit of telling myself. I can go ahead and exercise anyway." They don't get caught up in the excuse-filled chatter of the mental computer. They listen to excuses but follow through with exercise.

NOT NOW, SOMEDAY

Frank is the managing partner of a prosperous commercial real estate firm in the Southeast. He is a two-pack-a-day smoker, slightly overweight, suffering from high stress and getting insufficient exercise. He's following the all too frequent executive lifestyle —work hard, pay the price, and earn the big one (i.e., a heart attack). Frank's business partners are very concerned about his health. They ask me to speak to him. When I offer support, Frank responds, "It's not like I'm totally inactive. I get my share of exercise."

"What do you do?"

"I play tennis once a week and golf on weekends. Never fails."

"What percentage of the time do you spend in chasing balls and walking around, and not in vigorous volleying?"

"No, this is highly competitive tennis. We move around a lot."

"Aerobic conditioning and weight loss require at least three 30-minute workouts a week. Movement must be sustained for the entire 30 minutes. Golf doesn't qualify as aerobic. At best, you're getting one solid workout a week."

"I don't know when I could find the time to do more. Commuting to the country club is a problem during midweek traffic. Weeknights are for my family. I already get to work or to breakfast meetings by 7 o'clock."

"Frank, we're talking about finding one more hour a week for exercise. Are you willing to make a commitment to your physical well-being by setting aside that time?"

"Art, I appreciate your interest in my health but this phone call is making me late for important business matters. Thanks for talking to me and I'll let you know when I'm ready to make a commitment."

"That's exactly why we're having this conversation. Something more pressing always comes along and your health gets put on hold. My offer of support is interpreted as an intrusion on more important matters. Frank, your life is always going to be filled with new problems and opportunities. Waiting for the ideal time is actually a commitment to let your body decline. You see it as either a matter of your business or your health. Here's a new possibility. How about having it all—your business, family, and health?"

"Sounds wonderful in theory. I just don't feel this is a good time to start making changes with all the pressure I'm under. Maybe in a few months."

"If we waited for the time when you were free from business pressures, there's a good chance we'd wait for your retirement or death, whichever came first. Frank, if you knew you were doing something that put your business at risk for financial disaster, would you stop doing it immediately?"

"Of course, I'd take care of the problem."

"Then how can you tolerate allowing your health to decline. Aren't you the most important human resource in your business?"

Notice that Frank has become a prisoner of his own words. Unknowingly, Frank has appointed himself prison warden and is administering a life sentence to irregular exercise. This confinement is created by Frank's inner dialogue about the proper circumstances for exercise. It's not the demanding schedule that restricts Frank's activity.

Frank has fallen into the trap of "waiting for someday." His fitness depends on the right conditions turning up: when business problems disappear, when he feels less anxious, when early evening traffic jams vanish, or when time becomes available. What is the likelihood of all those conditions ever happening?

How about you? What conditions are you waiting for so you can get into the kind of shape you desire?

Stop reading for a few minutes. Write down the reasons you've used to explain why this isn't the right time to be exercising more regularly or with greater intensity.

_____

_____

_____

_____

_____

_____

Now, answer these three questions:

1. What's the likelihood these conditions will all be in place for any extended period of time?____

_____

2. If my exercise program hinges on these conditions being in place, what's the likelihood of my exercising regularly?_____

_____

3. What's my bottom line—having good reasons for putting off exercise, or being physically fit?____

_____

HOW WE HOLD COMMITMENTS— IN THE CLASS OF HOPES, DREAMS, AND GOOD IDEAS

Have you ever noticed that wanting something does not make much of a difference in the results? Often we have wants, desires, dreams, and goals, but they never go any farther. The gap between wants and results is caused by lack of action. For instance:

- You want a satisfying job but don't go looking for one.

- You want a satisfying relationship but don't approach members of the opposite sex.

- You want to stop smoking but you continue to buy cigarettes.

- You want to be rich but you don't want the responsibility and hard work that come with high-paying positions.

- You want to be fit, attractive, and healthy but you don't want to exercise.

Notice that wanting something means very little. Only action produces results. Being physically fit requires consistent exercise, not getting in shape one month and falling out of shape the next.

Most people will say they are "committed" to being fit and healthy. The problem is that we sometimes hold commitments in the same category as hopes, dreams, and good ideas. Commitment often means that we will pursue a goal so long as it isn't too difficult.

The distinction between true commitment and interest is action. True commitment shows up in our actions. Results are produced only through action.

You may be thinking, "Let's be realistic. Sometimes I feel committed but unforeseen circumstances stop me from exercising. Does commitment mean perfection?"

No, commitment is not perfection. In the absence of results, the committed exerciser does two things:

Step One: Accepts full responsibility for lack of results, rather than blaming circumstances.

Step Two: Makes an immediate correction. Missed workouts are promptly rescheduled. Advance planning takes into account travel time so that workout sessions don't get cut short. Excuses for coasting through a workout are not accepted.

Committed exercisers do what they say they'll do. When they find themselves off course, corrections get made promptly. Committed exercisers aren't satisfied with only dreaming about having a fit body. They know that the only way to convert dreams into reality is through action.

REASONS DON'T COUNT—RESULTS DO

One day while I was weight training, one of my fellow lifters said he had just quit smoking. I was startled that one of the gym regulars had been a three-pack-per-day smoker for ten years. I asked, "Why did you decide to quit now after thinking about stopping for all these years?" His answer was intriguing. "I didn't have any good reasons to continue smoking."

It is totally illogical for a decade-long smoking habit to end without any apparent reason and without struggle. Can it be possible that all it takes to break a habit is to say you will and really mean it?

One of my exercise clients, Dr. Ken Blanchard, is author of a best seller, *The One Minute Manager.*

For years Ken had wanted to get on a heavy-duty fitness regimen. Despite impressive starts, his exercise episodes were short-lived. New career opportunities, such as a videotape series, speaking engagements, publicity tours, and offers to write more books, would sabotage his fitness plans. Ken was frustrated. At a time when he had achieved financial independence, his children were in college, and his business was running smoothly, he felt he should have control of his schedule to make free time for exercise.

During our early fitness coaching sessions, I observed flashes of his reason-making process in Ken's weekly goal-setting. He said things like:

"I have several dinners with clients who will want to entertain me. It's not realistic to set a goal of no alcohol this week."

"I have a couple of coast-to-coast flights so I'll have to taper off to only three workouts instead of the usual five."

"We're staying with friends who are careful about what they eat so there won't be temptations to get off my diet."

"There are no morning seminars so I'll have clear sailing for six early-morning workouts."

Ken's goals were based on the circumstances of his life. Under favorable conditions, there was no compromising on his eating and exercise goals. However, goals were lowered at the appearance of difficulties.

Noticing this pattern, I remarked, "Ken, instead of basing goals on how the circumstances look, set your goals based on what works to get your desired fitness results. Instead of having good reasons to scale down goals, target an appropriate exercise level. We'll make plans to handle any unfavorable situations."

Ken's choice was clear. As he put it, "Either I get bigger than my reasons, or I get bigger." And Ken got smaller—nearly forty pounds lighter during our year of working together.

Committed exercisers are unreasonable with their reasons for not exercising. They refuse to tolerate any reasons for prolonged breaks in a routine. They are able to come up with a hundred reasons for not exercising and still do it anyway.

Overcome your tendency to be reasonable by exercising even when it seems too difficult. If fatigue at day's end seems to rule out exercise, go out for a brisk ten-minute walk just to prove you can do it. Watch out—You may feel more energetic after ten minutes and want to go farther.

Perhaps you've claimed that raising young children prevents going to aerobics classes. Go buy an exercise videotape. Invite a workout partner to your home. Move your body while keeping an eye on the kids.

Do hassles with your boyfriend, girlfriend, or spouse leave you too depressed to get a good workout? Go do it anyway. Prove you can exercise even when you don't feel like doing it.

One by one, good reasons for not exercising will be sapped of their power. What seems unreasonable becomes easy and routine. Circumstances in your life don't have to change in order for you to get consistent exercise. By going ahead and exercising, you'll find your perceptions of difficulty become weakened. Suddenly you will create all the motivation you'll ever need to be a regular exerciser.

The Easy-Way-Out Traps

Fitness motivator: "How come you've been away from exercise for six months?"

Client: "My wife is pregnant."

Fitness motivator: "What!"

Client: "Well, I don't think it would be right for me to get trim and look great while she's growing heavier. This situation requires some compassion. I call it 'sympathy obesity.'"

Moral: There is no end to the variety of excuses for not exercising.

Sam Strider is a young executive. His career is taking off. Unfortunately, his fitness program is winding down.

For years Sam has been a regular jogger and racquetball player, even entering tournaments and 10K runs. Five hours of exercise a week was routine. Sam often inspired his business associates to be physically active.

How could this fitness buff become a weekend jock? Career success has required breakfast meetings, increased travel, entertaining major accounts, and bringing home paperwork. Arriving home late and exhausted, Sam wants to eat and rest. Exercise is the last thing he feels like doing. Sam already misses time with his family. Where is he going to find time to exercise regularly?

Sound familiar? Frustrating, isn't it? The familiarity of this cycle may prevent you from noticing your own role in causing an exercise slump. It looks like unavoidable circumstances are stopping you from exercising consistently. The real saboteur is your own thinking.

Your thinking falls into the pattern of "Here's why I can't possibly exercise." These automatic reminders of difficulties are called *The Easy-Way-Out Traps*.

These traps are very subtle. They enable us to rationalize that we would exercise except for unfavorable circumstances. We feel justified in not making the extra effort to exercise.

This chapter will help you become an expert in spotting your own brand of Easy-Way-Out Traps before they upset your exercise plans. Right now, the traps appear to be the only way to assess the situation. You almost have to be knocked on the head so that you don't succumb to them.

A breakthrough comes when you treat the traps for what they really are—perceptions of difficulty that you're making up. They are not legitimate barriers to exercise.

```
┌─────────────────────────────────────────────┐
│                                             │
│       The Four Easy-Way-Out Traps           │
│                                             │
│     1. The immediate satisfaction trap      │
│                                             │
│     2. The short-term goals trap            │
│                                             │
│     3. The "I've got good reasons" trap     │
│                                             │
│     4. The permanent failure trap           │
│                                             │
└─────────────────────────────────────────────┘
```

THE IMMEDIATE SATISFACTION TRAP

When we consider doing something difficult, we tend to focus on the immediate consequences and ignore the long-range results. What we expect to be immediately in store for us has greater impact on our decisions than those benefits that may or may not happen in the distant future.

Here's how the immediate satisfaction trap works. Imagine you are returning to your exercise routine after a few weeks layoff. You've scheduled an appointment with a fitness instructor for a personal workout session. Your workout gear was packed the night before. The children are staying at the neighbor's house. And it's Monday, the day that most Americans start exercise programs and diets. Perfect conditions for an exercise comeback are in place.

Fifteen minutes before it's time to leave for your workout, the immediate satisfaction trap takes over. You're thinking, "I didn't get a good night's sleep and

I'm feeling tired. I'm certain to feel weak and out of breath. The fitness instructor will show no mercy. I don't feel like being pushed tonight. After all, it's important to feel psyched up the first time back or else I'm sure to drop out again. I'll try again next Monday."

The immediate satisfaction trap springs again. What looked like perfect conditions for getting back to the gym are replaced by fresh perceptions of difficulty. At the moment of choice, it feels better to miss the workout and avoid feeling winded, tired, and pressured. Besides, staying home allows you to watch Dynasty on TV. That clinches it. No exercise tonight.

Notice that this decision is based entirely on *what feels better* at the moment instead of *what works* for long-term fitness results. No wonder people go on and go off exercise programs when doing it depends on their feelings at any moment. Sometimes you'll feel like exercising and sometimes you won't. What is the likelihood of consistent exercise when doing it depends on always feeling psyched, excited, and enthusiastic?

Whoever said we have to feel good in order to do something? We act as if it's a hard and fast rule of human behavior. We place tremendous importance on feeling good before we can take action.

The irony is that only action produces results. Exercising gets people in shape. Your feelings don't make any difference. Do you want to spend your life chasing after good feelings or being physically fit?

Committed exercisers know they don't have to feel like exercising to do it. They are committed to getting lasting fitness results instead of having good feelings for the moment.

You can break free of this unconscious link between your feelings and your actions. In fact, you've done it in many situations. Which of these have ever applied to you?

- You don't feel like going to work, yet you go anyway.
- You feel stressed by your children and don't feel like cooking, yet you prepare the meal.
- You feel like eating chocolate mousse, yet you order a piece of cantaloupe. (I never said *all* of these would fit for you).

Commitment is the common element in all these situations that enables you to act in disregard for your feelings. The commitment to provide for family keeps us going to work and cooking their favorite meals. The commitment to permanent weight control is what causes people to stick with diets, even when tempted by wonderful desserts.

So what about exercise? Isn't it interesting that when it comes to your health your feelings are allowed to call the shots? Commitment makes the difference. Once you are committed to a goal, you lose the freedom to act based on how you feel. Actions, not feelings, are what count when it comes down to producing results.

THE SHORT-TERM GOAL TRAP

The words used to describe goals can set us up to fail. This trap involves setting goals that target only short-term results when long-term results are really desired. Unfortunately, the good intentions that motivate us to begin exercising will later set us up to quit when difficulties arise.

An example of this trap is using special events to target exercise goals. For instance, you might say:

"The high school reunion is in six weeks. I've got to look my best. If I'm going to fit into my formal wear, the extra pounds must come off real fast."

"The company picnic is coming up. My thighs are looking heavy. I don't want to feel self-conscious parading around in shorts. If I'm going to last through a few games of volleyball, it's time for a crash fitness program."

"I've got to finish this 10K run so that everyone on our office team completes the event."

What happens when the class reunion, the company picnic, or the 10K run is over? Most of us go right back to our old eating and exercise habits. Good intentions caused a short-lived burst of exercise. However, lasting fitness results are what we really want.

We also think short-term when we "try" an exercise program. If we like it, we'll stick with it. The focus is on our feelings about the activity, not on lasting results.

Let's say you agree to try an aerobic dance class. You take your position in line with the other participants. The first song leads to a shocking discovery—your body refuses to move to the music of Lionel Richie. Then when the Pointer Sisters sing "I'm So Excited," and get to the verse "I'm about to lose control and I think I like it," you think it's the kind of song that's corrupting the morals of America. In fact, you prefer Lawrence Welk to rock. At that point, it's all right to leave because you did what you'd intended. You tried aerobic dance and you didn't like it. It doesn't matter that the exercise would be great for the muscle toning you originally had in mind. You immediately dismissed it, without even checking to find whether other classes featured more appealing music. Your participation was based on "liking it," not on desired results.

Most of us operate as if exercise must always be enjoyable or else we don't have to do it. This standard is rarely applied in other areas of our lives. For instance, when our jobs are dull or stressful for months at a time we don't just quit. A few boring days with a spouse doesn't constitute grounds for divorce. Somehow, exercise is expected to be always enjoyable. If not, we have sufficient reason to stop. Short-term experimenting with fitness programs robs us of lasting results.

The trap of saying you'll "try" to do something is similar to saying you'll "go on" an exercise program. What does "going on" imply? That someday you'll go off.

In the United States, we tend to go on and off exercise programs in mass unison. We have a national grace period that begins on Thanksgiving Day and runs until New Year's Day. Our motto then is "eat, drink, and be merry." Most of us take advantage of this opportunity for a reprieve from diets and exercise without feeling the least bit guilty. "'Tis the season to be jolly" and exercise just doesn't seem to fit. We turn six days of holiday into a six-week siesta from fitness.

What happens on January 2 after the college bowl games are over? It's time to make New Year's resolutions to get back in shape. Most people "go on" exercise programs and diets to lose their extra weight quickly so they can return to eating, drinking, and being merry.

The short-term intentions that get us started in exercise all too often lead us to dropping out. "Trying" and "going on" exercise programs is not the kind of language that indicates commitment. Our initial exercise efforts might bring fast results but we quickly return to a less active lifestyle.

Steering clear of this trap begins with stating

goals in words that describe long-term results. There can be no more trying, wanting, hoping, or even giving it your best shot. Only promises and commitments will work. We will talk more about setting goals in Chapter 6.

THE "I'VE GOT GOOD REASONS" TRAP

The mind of an interested exerciser operates as if it were both a lawyer and a jury. As the lawyer, it prepares a case filled with persuasive reasons for staying inactive. As the jury, it rules "not guilty" for not exercising. As long as there is enough evidence of good reasons, we accept our current performance even if it means settling for mediocre fitness.

Reasons for avoiding exercise are endless. Study the following collection of good reasons. Circle the ones you use from time to time.

Here's What's Wrong With Exercise

I know I should exercise but . . .

- It's too painful.
- It makes me tired, sweaty, winded.
- It reminds me of how out of shape I am.
- It's boring.
- If I ever stop, I'll lose whatever I've gained (I'll put back the weight, lose endurance, my muscle will turn to fat).

- I'll have to do it for the rest of my life.
- I'll be the unlucky one who suffers shinsplints, strains my back, etc.
- It's too great a sacrifice.
- It's unproductive. It's silly to push myself to run/ lift weights/swim laps, etc.

The Old Faithfuls: Time and Money

I know I should exercise but . . .

- Something always comes up when I want to do it.
- I can't find the time.
- My family will never give me the time.
- It costs too much for home equipment/gym membership fee.
- It takes too long to notice any results.
- It's not the right time (too cold in winter, kids home in summer, busy season at work).
- If I lose weight, I won't be able to afford a new wardrobe.
- If I put on muscle, I won't be able to buy normal size clothes. I can't afford custom-made clothes.

It's Not For Me

I know I should exercise but . . .

- I'm a terrible procrastinator.
- I'm not the athletic type.
- I just can't seem to get started.
- I don't know what keeps me from exercising.
- I can't bring myself to do it consistently.
- I come from a nonathletic family.
- It's not very ladylike.
- I'm in good enough shape without it.
- I'm too far out of shape.
- I get enough exercise at work/doing housework/ caring for kids.
- I'm too tired after a hard day.
- I'm basically lazy.
- I'm not graceful and coordinated.
- I'm not sure I'll get the results I want.
- I can't diet and exercise at the same time. It's too much.
- I just want to lose weight. My diet will take off the extra pounds.
- I've never been sick a day in my life.
- I'm not the heart attack type.

- I drink, smoke, and eat too much.
- I've tried before but never stuck with it.
- I'm not sure I'm motivated enough.
- I lack willpower/discipline.
- I can't do it by myself. I need a workout partner.
- I hate to structure my time for exercise.
- I want to have fun. There are things that are more fun to do than exercise.

All lined up like this, these reasons may seem flimsy. But in real life, they can be so persuasive.

Committed exercisers are unreasonable in regard to any reasons for missing workouts (except when working out would aggravate injuries and illness). At the moment of choice, they know there's only one question that matters:

What's it going to be—reasons or results?

THE PERMANENT FAILURE TRAP

This is the most fatal of all the Easy-Way-Out Traps, because it kills the possibility of ever having a physically fit lifestyle. The permanent failure trap operates when we decide that regular exercise is impossible based on past failures to stick with exercise. We treat the past as if it were a reliable measure of our best effort.

Sometimes just a few unpleasant experiences can cause a lingering dislike for exercise. Consider the middle-aged executive who was once a skinny little kid and always got picked last whenever teams were chosen in gym class. He concludes that he's a lifetime wimp, hangs up his jockstrap, and retires from physical activities. It's safer for the old ego to stay in the boardroom than to venture into the locker room.

Until recently, few women were exposed to organized team sports. As girls, women had received strong messages to avoid physical exertion: *Sweating isn't ladylike. Sports are for tomboys. Women are the weaker sex.* Early messages can become permanent prohibitions stored in the mental computer.

Once a bad track record is established, we notice many drawbacks and few rewards for exercising. We feel defeated. We conclude that the fitness revolution will have to go on with us on the sidelines.

Get released from the permanent failure trap. Give yourself a fresh start with exercise. Don't view your past to predict what will happen now.

Past history has no bearing on future performance. You've undoubtedly heard about elderly people who for decades were month-on, month-off exercisers yet suddenly embarked on a daily walking program. Somehow they never miss a day of walking. It defies logic that such an abrupt change can happen. Isn't it supposed to be more difficult to change a habit as we get older? However, commitment is not logical. Changing your exercise pattern is possible at any moment, regardless of past history.

As long as you are taking action, failure is impossible. The only way to fail is to give up: Refuse to ever set foot in a gym again. Put on a bathing suit only to get a suntan. Bury your rowing machine under boxes in the far corner of your closet.

By returning to your exercise program, even after long slumps, you are not failing. You are in the process of winning.

BREAKING FREE OF THE EASY-WAY-OUT TRAPS

Awareness of the Easy-Way-Out Traps will not make them go away. They will continue to come up

**THE BIG SHIFT IN PERCEPTIONS
OF DIFFICULTY**

Interested	Committed
1. Feelings control actions (the immediate satisfaction trap)	1. Actions based on what works
2. Short-term and tentative start-up goals (the short-term goals trap)	2. Goals stated as firm promises and revised periodically
3. Reasons created to account for lack of results (the "I've got good reasons" trap)	3. Being unreasonable with reasons for not exercising
4. Use of past history of poor results to predict failure (the permanent failure trap)	4. Recognition that poor results in the past have no bearing on current performance

when you consider exercising. The key difference will be in how you treat the traps. Instead of seeing them as unsolvable barriers, recognize that they are only perceptions of difficulty. They are just words you are in the habit of saying to yourself about the difficulties of staying fit. When you move from being interested to being committed to physical fitness, your perception of the traps changes.

This power to dispute the Easy-Way-Out Traps is always available in the presence of commitment.

You have the power to go and exercise regardless of whether you feel like it or not.

You have the power to go and exercise even when you have good reasons for not exercising.

You have the power to set firm long-term goals and get lasting results.

You have the power at every instant to be the physically active person you wish to be, regardless of your past history with exercise.

Your Body is Built to Be Exercised

We are warned to get a doctor's approval before starting an exercise program. Maybe we really need a doctor's approval for staying inactive.

Do you want to always be self-conscious about being somewhat overweight? Do you want to always be preoccupied with wondering if others are noticing your chunky thighs and pot belly?

Do you want to start showing signs of old age earlier than you need to?

Do you want to put your body at risk for health breakdowns?

Do you want to feel worn out and to lack energy for the things you want to do?

Of course you'd answer "no" to each question. But when you exercise irregularly, your actions are actually saying "yes."

You want the benefits that exercise makes possible. What stops you from fully enjoying these benefits is the extra effort required.

How can you adjust your thinking so that the benefits of exercise are more compelling than the effort to do it? The basic strategy is to focus on ways that being fit can improve the quality of your life right now. Not twenty, thirty, or forty years from now, but each and every day you live. This shift can be more easily accomplished once you are convinced of one simple fact.

Your body was built to be exercised. If an owner's manual came with your body at birth, its basic instruction would be three words long:
MOVE IT—REGULARLY!

In the last chapter, the Easy-Way-Out Traps were exposed as perceptions of difficulty rather than as legitimate reasons for curtailing exercise. Their influence was weakened. However, the job of becoming a committed exerciser is only partially done. We also have to increase the value of being fit.

Here's a tip: *Focus on the benefits of being physically fit instead of on the activity of exercise.* How would fitness improve the quality of your family life, your career, and your leisure time? Picture yourself being able to count on the vitality to go after your dreams at 100 percent effort. Gradually, exercise ceases to be something you must force yourself to do. It becomes a natural choice because the benefits are worth it.

USE IT OR LOSE IT

Energy is a commodity that is more valuable than gold, real estate, or even a new BMW. Energy is fuel for an active and productive life. Imagine the attractive opportunities you give up on with the reply, "No, I'm too tired." What if conserving energy weren't a concern? What if you could say "yes" to new opportunities all the time? Your life would look very different.

Do you want your life to resemble a slow motion movie in which you consciously have to pace yourself to get through the workday? How much of your evening time is now spent confined to your easy chair recovering from the exhaustion of a day's activities? Four hours? If that's the case, you may be losing one fourth of your waking hours.

Imagine the difference it would make if you could go full tilt, knowing you could always count on having enough energy. It's your choice. You can feel tired just looking at a busy appointment calendar (even a month in advance). Or you can approach each day confident that you can handle a demanding schedule and take advantage of your opportunities.

If I were offering a drug that immediately raised your energy whenever you were dragging, there would be lots of buyers. Actually, I am offering that drug. It's called exercise. Paradoxically, your body is energized by working harder.

If you exercise sporadically, you may recall the beginning of an exercise program to be tiring, not energizing. But that feeling was only a sign you were out of shape. The fatigue is temporary. As the body gets into shape, vigorous and sustained movement triggers an upsurge of energy.

Treat your body as it was meant to be treated. Give it mild exertion. Feel the burst of energy. Enjoy a new aliveness.

EXERCISE KEEPS YOU YOUNG

Much of what we call aging is not caused by the wear of activity but by lack of use. We assume that physical effort wears down the body. Instead, the body is rejuvenated by being worked harder.

Physiologically, the effects of aging and disuse are indistinguishable. This is why it's so easy to attribute physical decline to growing old. However, the fifty-year-old who says, "I can't do now what I could at 30" is often using age as an excuse. Most of the loss of physical ability has nothing to do with aging. For fully trained exercisers, the loss of physical condition and strength is only 12 to 15 percent from age twenty-one to age sixty.

John Jerome, an expert on the physiology of aging and author of *The Sweet Spot in Time,* maintains that the best way to keep the body young is to work it. First, regular exercise mildly stresses the heart so this all-important muscle grows bigger and stronger. It pumps more blood with each beat, which allows it to slow down and relax on routine activities. The heart functions more efficiently when we regularly work it harder.

Second, systematic stress to bone stimulates the laying down of calcium and other structural components that make the bones grow stronger, thereby helping to prevent osteoporosis. The frail and weak bones of older people are often due to inactivity, not just aging.

Finally, exercise keeps muscles toned. We're all familiar with the shriveling up and wasting away of muscles when placed in a cast. If a muscle is immobilized for a few weeks and withers away noticeably, consider the effects of *years* of inactivity. Our muscles were built for movement and lifting, not for constantly sitting and lying around.

Yet our culture gives clear messages to slow down and age "gracefully." In most cases, "slow down" is translated "stop completely." Many of us spend our lives resting, thinking we're preserving our youth. We are actually hastening the aging and decline of the body.

Stop blaming Father Time for the body's wearing down when inactivity is the real culprit.

It's a mistake to think you're too old to exercise. We're all familiar with people who go on exercise programs after years of inactivity and suddenly look ten years younger. Regardless of your age or the time since you were physically active, you can get back lots of the physiological vitality of youth. Get started now. Don't be like the person who once said, "If I had known I was going to live this long I would have started taking care of myself years ago."

We spend huge sums of money on cosmetics and clothing to look and feel youthful. Actually, the best investment is to maintain a fit and healthy body. "Cosmetic fitness" looks good but there's nothing like the real thing. Imagine how great it will feel in your senior years when you can announce your age with pride because your energy and appearance are so exceptional.

EXERCISE AND LONGER LIFE

Dr. Ralph Paffenburger and his associates at Stanford have done the most extensive study of the connection between exercise and longevity. The study followed 17,000 males who entered Harvard from 1916 to 1950. The researchers concluded that for each hour of exercise, we can expect to live that hour over, perhaps with another one to two hours extra. Subjects who walked nine miles a week had 21 percent lower death rate than those who walked three miles a week or less. Three or four workouts a week for a lifetime reduce the negative effects of smoking, high blood pressure, and some genetic factors. Paffenburger concluded that the benefits of steady exercise are comparable to those that come with medical breakthroughs, bringing in some cases life extensions of twenty years.

PERMANENT WEIGHT CONTROL

Have you ever wondered why there are so many diet books on the market? Because they don't work. While excess weight comes off in the early stages of dieting, it often all eventually comes back, sometimes with a few extra pounds for good measure. When one diet doesn't work, we assume it's because we didn't pick the right diet, and the search continues. Stop throwing away your money on diet books and exotic weight loss foods. Lack of exercise is the real problem.

Even if you are eating a low calorie, low fat diet, you have to include exercise to achieve permanent weight control. Since your body was built to be exercised, it is difficult to maintain proper body weight without it.

Some people, especially seasoned dieters, will argue that exercise doesn't burn enough calories to justify all the effort. They look at charts of calories expended in exercise and get depressed. If twenty minutes of brisk walking burns only 100 calories, how many hours will it take to burn off an extra helping of a Sara Lee chocolate cream pie? Does this mean that I can't work off the exotic dinner on Friday night with a weekend of tennis (160 calories expended/20 minutes) and golf (90 calories expended/ 20 minutes)? It may appear that you need to become a triathlete or a marathoner to burn off enough calories through exercise.

But exercise makes a big difference because it changes the way your body burns calories. A diet with no exercise results in equal loss of fat and muscle tissue. Add exercise and the weight loss will be about 80 percent fat and only 20 percent muscle. When your body is lean, your metabolism burns more calories all the time, even while you are inactive. You could be burning calories while sitting at your desk reading this book.

Dieting alone doesn't work for permanent weight control. Exercise is essential to trim down, and to *keep off* excess pounds and inches. How much aggravation have you endured trying to lose weight through dieting alone? How important is it for you to look attractive? Being overweight increases the risk of heart attacks and diabetes. The American Medical Association reports a 35 percent increase in the death rate for people 20 percent overweight. How important is your health? If your weight has been a long-standing concern for you, commit yourself to the winning formula: *Diet + Exercise.*

LOOKING GOOD

A primary reason people get started with exercise is to improve their appearance. The desire to have a well-proportioned body with well-toned muscles is a strong motivator. Most people have one or two specific areas from which they're eager to take off extra fat. Women are especially concerned about hips and thighs, and many men are plagued by bulging bellies.

People often assume that if they overexercise a fat area, it will get trimmer. Doing hundreds of leg raises and donkey kicks to counter flabby thighs is a waste of time. Doing sit-ups will keep you busy, but don't expect to take inches off your stomach. Unfortunately, "spot reducing" is doomed to fail.

Subcutaneous fat is found beneath the skin. It can be seen and pinched. But it cannot be reduced from a select spot on the body. In fact, overexercising a specific muscle group will probably create a layer of muscle to go along with the fat already there.

So where does exercise fit in the battle of the bulges? Subcutaneous fat is burned for fuel when the demand for calories is great. Therefore, the best strategy is to give up spot reducing and go for a total body exercise program, such as walking, swimming, or running. When you exercise large muscle groups, you create a demand for calories and draw the fat from all parts of the body. Once you've cut down to desired proportions by burning the top layer of subcutaneous fat, exercising specific body parts will then firm up and tone the muscles.

Don't get caught up in the quick fix mentality of overexercising fat areas in hopes of spot reducing. Get the full body in motion to burn maximum calories and the fat will gradually come off those troublesome areas. Be patient, exercise the full body, and you'll look great.

SLEEPING SOUNDLY

I've been amazed by the number of people in my seminars who report having difficulty sleeping. It's interesting to find out their activity level. The inactive people can stay in bed for ten hours yet feel sluggish the next day. Often their sleep period is spent tossing and turning, without deep relaxation. However, physically active people often sleep much less than the eight-hour average, yet stay wide awake all day. They hit the bed and within five minutes, they're sound asleep. Upon rising in the morning, they feel refreshed.

Sounder sleep is one of the first physical benefits reported by people starting up exercise programs. Exercise relaxes your body, sleep comes naturally, and you are quickly re-energized.

DISSOLVING STRESS THROUGH REGULAR EXERCISE

The last few decades have produced many techniques for managing stress: flotation tanks, biofeedback, meditation, yoga, massage, even retreating to romance novels. For most people, stress management has become associated with learning how to relax. Actually, stress management through physical exertion works just as well.

Exercise reduces stress in three ways. First, a fit body is better able to withstand the internal wear and tear that occurs under stress. Stress prepares the body to confront danger by "fight or flight." The automatic response to stress includes rapid breathing, sweating, surging adrenalin, tensing muscles, and brisk pumping of the heart. If it happens frequently, this physical arousal can damage internal organs. For a well-conditioned person, the fight-or-flight response has less dramatic physiological effects. For example, in a physically fit individual, the heart rate stays lower and rises more slowly when stress occurs.

A second benefit is that exercise provides a needed change of pace from the often sedentary and mental activity of work to physical activity. When exercise is done after work, it is a wonderful transition into your personal life. It's a great way to leave the office behind. The hour spent on exercise is really a way of treating yourself. It's a time to release frustrations and tensions, and to rejuvenate yourself to make the most of each evening. It's like capturing a second wind to complete the day.

Finally, exercise is a natural tranquilizer. A sustained period of exercise causes secretion of a hormone called endorphin, which has a calming effect on the body. (Endorphin is also released when you have a burst of laughter.) Endorphin causes the "runner's high" which can occur after thirty to forty minutes of jogging.

If you do nothing else to manage stress but to get on a regular exercise program, you are doing something extremely beneficial.

SHAPING UP YOUR LOVE LIFE

Not many things are as important to you as your love life. The search to improve sexual satisfaction can include books on lovemaking, therapy to get at the root of sexual problems, plastic surgery to create a sexier appearance, trips to romantic places, and even exotic paraphernalia and skin oils. But with all the means that exist to improve your love life, one basic fact remains—sex is a physical act.

Sexual performance involves strength, flexibility, endurance, and tone. Strength in the limbs, stomach, pelvic region, legs, back, and neck ensure ease of sexual movements. Flexibility allows initiating and reacting to whatever delightful maneuvers you or your partner dream up. Muscle tone enhances sex appeal. It may be a turn-on for your partner to look at and touch a firm, well-toned body. Finally, endurance is critical so that your body doesn't weaken while your passion still lingers.

Having a fit body also increases self-confidence as a lover. It's hard to be sexy when you're worried about whether your partner will be turned off by your bare body or whether you'll be able to keep up the pace. Being in shape eliminates these worries. A fit body certainly leads to greater pleasure in the bedroom.

RELIEVING BACK PAIN

Have you ever noticed the high frequency of back pain reported by people with pot bellies? It's no coincidence. The extra weight in the stomach puts strain on the lower back muscles supporting the spine. Getting rid of the strain means losing the paunch.

A weak back places some restrictions on the form of exercise a person should start with, but is not a reason to stay inactive. While running may aggravate a bad back, walking, swimming, or cycling won't. These exercises are great calorie burners and in combination with a proper diet will soon trim down the gut.

A calisthenics program designed to strengthen the back muscles is also necessary. Sit-ups in which knees are brought up to the chest are excellent for back pain, as are toe touching and trunk circles. If you have back pain, get an exercise prescription from a physical therapist or exercise physiologist.

Enduring chronic back pain is no way to go

through life. The solution to getting rid of such pain and the related physical limitations is exercise.

ACHIEVING PERSONAL EXCELLENCE

Many regular exercisers claim that the greatest rewards of exercise are the mental skills that it enhances—skills that bring success in many areas of life. The physical fitness arena is a perfect training ground because the results are so visible and measurable. It is very inspiring to see positive changes in speed, strength, endurance, flexibility, body weight, body fat, blood pressure, or waist size. Body changes thought to be in the hands of uncontrollable forces, such as aging, turn out to be under our own control. If such dramatic results can be produced with the body, then change is possible everywhere.

Here's an example of how exercise breakthroughs are often transferred to one's job or personal life. Jerry has sold business equipment for about five years. His annual sales figures were very stable, ranking in the middle of those of a sales force of 100. Jerry was content to be making the same commission check year after year. After all, significantly increasing sales require lots of extra effort. Besides, there was no guarantee that if he became one of the company's sales champions for one year he'd be able to do it again. No sense in raising the boss's expectations.

Jerry's pattern with exercise was similar to his sales performance. While he'd never been totally inactive, one or two workouts a week hadn't made him a perfect physical specimen. Jerry rationalized that getting in better shape would take too much time and effort. Besides, why press himself to top flight fitness, when he's rarely sick and he still puts in a strong day's work (until 3 o'clock, anyway)?

One day, Jerry's sales manager was taken to the hospital for emergency treatment. It was diagnosed as a mild heart attack. The sales manager was only thirty-five years old. He survived but his pace at work would never be the same. Jerry was scared by his boss's close brush with death. Within days, he called me for an appointment to begin upgrading his exercise program. I remember thinking, "Isn't it sad that people have to see their health decline or notice it in a close friend, to get motivated for exercise."

Our goal was to get Jerry's exercise level up to four workouts a week and to have him lose ten pounds. Jerry did everything I asked of him. Each Sunday night Jerry wrote down his weekly exercise goals, and reviewed them daily. He created time to add on two or three workouts each week. His schedule wasn't nearly as packed as he'd imagined. He trained vigorously in his jogging program and in weight lifting. Instead of merely going through the motions, Jerry pressed himself to run faster or to increase weight on the barbells. Even when Jerry felt depressed, he'd stick with his scheduled fitness program. There was no stopping his climb to high-level fitness. Ultimately, Jerry entered a 10K race and placed in the top 10 percent for his age group.

One day I asked Jerry, "How're sales going?"

"Glad you asked," he replied. "Lots of what we're doing with exercise seems to have rubbed off. For the first time, I'm doing weekly goal-setting and reviewing goals daily. Instead of my productivity declining after 3 P.M., my energy remains high until bedtime. I'm making more sales calls and profits are rising. I'm shortening periods of sales declines by not letting my unpleasant feelings be a reason for cutting down effort. I'm going to make the top 10 percent and qualify for the sales champions group. Everything's coming together."

The self-management skills learned or reinforced through participation in a regular fitness program include:

- *Goal-setting.* In all areas of life, goal-setting gives direction for achieving results.

- *Hard work.* Paying the price of extra effort transfers easily to one's career, school, or relationships.

- *Self-responsibility.* Only you can be responsible for exercising. No one else can do the sit-ups, peddle the exercise bike, or swim the laps for you. This sense of personal responsibility for fitness carries over to a responsibility for producing results in other areas.

- *Persistence.* Physical fitness is not a quick fix. It requires lifelong commitment. Persistence in the face of inevitable difficulties is a quality of all successful people.

THE WEALTH OF EXERCISE BENEFITS

Irregular exercisers focus on the inconvenience and physical discomfort of exercise. Regular exercisers focus on the benefits of exercise—constant reminders that the extra effort is worth it.

Here is a list of appearance, fitness, health, psychological, and financial benefits. Most of these results will become noticeable within the first month of a fitness program. As you read through the list, check off the benefits you find most appealing.

Appearance Benefits

- Improve body symmetry, redistribute weight
- Firm and tone muscles
- Maintain proper body weight
- Appear younger, more attractive
- Walk taller, stand straighter

Physical Fitness Benefits

- Increase energy, stamina, and vitality
- Increase muscle strength and endurance
- Improve coordination and reflexes
- Increase suppleness and flexibility
- Retard muscle atrophy (loss of firmness, wasting away)

Health Benefits

- Reduce body fat content
- Stimulate circulation, strengthen heart
- Sleep more soundly; less need for sleep
- Increase resistance to illness and disease
- Relieve tension and stress
- Decrease risk of heart attack
- Live longer
- Decrease smoking, drinking, overeating
- Slow down the aging process
- Prevent being overweight
- Reduce lower back pain

Psychological and Performance Benefits

- Work harder without becoming fatigued
- Sharpen skills for sports and recreation
- Learn self-discipline
- Increase mental alertness and concentration
- Feel better about yourself; increase self-esteem and confidence
- Feel pride of being physically fit
- Feel less stressed, more relaxed
- Feel more control over your life
- Improve sex life

Financial Benefits

- Reduce bills/costs for medical care
- Reduce insurance premiums
- Fit into old wardrobe; save on expense of new clothes

Let's take stock of the value you place on being physically fit. In reading this chapter, what new benefits have you learned? Which ones have been reinforced? Review the checklist and write down the three most important benefits and why they are so important.

Benefits:	*Why benefit is important to me:*
1. _____	1. _____
_____	_____
2. _____	2. _____
_____	_____
3. _____	3. _____
_____	_____

Exercise is a gift that keeps on giving. Each workout is an opportunity to treat yourself to these impressive benefits. You're not only staying healthy but upgrading the overall quality of your life. It's incredible how a few hours a week of exercise can make such a difference.

Motivation Training Sessions

> "A workout is 25 percent PERSPIRA-
> TION and 75 percent DETERMINATION."
>
> —George Allen,
>   Former Coach of the
>   Washington Redskins and
>   Chairman of the
>   President's Council on
>   Physical Fitness and Sports

Habit change is difficult and takes a long time. We all know that old behavior patterns don't just change overnight. . . .

Hold on. Let's examine that belief for a moment. There is evidence that habit change can be easy and quick.

Take the case of a seasoned bachelor who has always kept living quarters that would never receive the *Good Housekeeping* Seal of Approval. Except when his parents visit, the garbage is piled high, dirty dishes fill the kitchen, whiskers speckle the bathroom sink, and guests tiptoe through the jock-straps and gym shorts on the living room rug. Then he changes from hopeless slob to neat housekeeper. How do we explain the transformation that just seems to happen one day?

Consider the out-of-shape, overweight company president who is constantly staging comebacks with his exercise program. It looks as though a fit lifestyle is on hold until retirement. All of a sudden, motivation seems to strike. He instructs his secretary to schedule exercise periods in his appointment calendar. Convenient workout facilities seem to be everywhere he travels. The airlines have special menus to fit his low-fat diet. Within six months, he's running every morning before work. He sponsors a companywide corporate fitness program, and challenges senior management to either get in shape or forget about promotions.

How do we account for these brisk and easy habit changes? Incredible turn of events? Exceptional cases? Not at all. The common factor is a shift from interest to commitment. The bachelor stops "trying" to keep a clean home and gets committed to having an impeccable living space. The company president who's been interested in exercise, commits to a fit lifestyle now before his health suffers. The cutting edge for habit change is *commitment.* Merely trying, wanting, and being interested don't cut it.

In my exercise motivation seminars, people often ask me:

"Where does commitment come from? Does it just appear out of thin air?"

"How do you go about declaring a commitment? I've made New Year's resolutions before—is this something different?"

"I've felt fired up about exercise before. How is this time going to be any different from all the other false starts?"

You're not only going to get the answers to these questions, but will learn the step-by-step blueprint for success used in my motivation seminars.

This chapter consists of a series of motivation training sessions that will guide you in making a commitment. Even more important, they will show you how to stay committed, not for a month but for the rest of your life.

Here is an outline of the steps of the motivation training sessions:

Step 1: Creating a picture of "a body that works"

Step 2: Taking responsibility for exercise slumps

Step 3: Creating an inspiring purpose for your fitness commitment

Step 4: Examining the risks of your fitness commitment

Step 5: Setting goals and monitoring progress

Step 6: Receiving support from your motivational coach

Step 7: Preparing for weak moments

Step 8: Making your workout fun

The first four steps of motivation training prepare you to launch your exercise program. They are the foundation of a lasting commitment.

Steps 5–8 are done weekly and daily. They sustain your commitment inspite of unanticipated difficulties that are bound to emerge. By being rigorous in these sessions you develop new mental habits to handle any and all Easy-Way-Out Traps.

To get the most out of each motivation training session, take out a pencil and answer the questions in the spaces provided. Don't attempt to quickly read through the book hoping to feel motivated by the final page. Mastering self-motivation involves learning new mental skills. Take the time to practice. Go for results, not speed. The payoff in increased fitness will be worth it.

STEP 1: CREATING A PICTURE OF "A BODY THAT WORKS"

The clearer the image you have of the result, the greater the likelihood you will achieve it. Vivid pictures stir up positive feelings and motivation for goal achievement.

MOTIVATION TRAINING SESSION: PICTURING A BODY THAT WORKS

Time: One or more ten-minute periods.

Purpose: To create a mental picture of the results you want to achieve through regular exercise.

Have fun with this exercise. In the space provided, write down whatever associations come to mind in response to the following questions. Let your imagination run wild. As images or words come to mind, immediately jot them down on paper. It may be helpful to find a quiet place and close your eyes to conjure up the most vivid images.

1. What images come to mind when you think of "a body that works"? Stay with this phrase for a few minutes and keep looking for images to add to your list. Go for quantity.

2. Recall when you were in the best shape of your life. What did your body look like then? What physical performance were you capable of? Which of these images of your top physical condition would you like to regain?

3. How would improved physical fitness pay off in your work performance? Your hobbies? Your relationships with family and friends? Your recreational activities?

4. Recall a time when working out or participating in your favorite sport was especially fun. What was your experience like? What if you could duplicate that experience once again?

One of my clients came up with this list:

> ### A Body that Works
>
> Alignment of physical, mental, spiritual
>
> | | |
> |---|---|
> | Healthy | Strong |
> | Feminine | Not skinny, not fat |
> | Graceful | Flexible |
> | Very attractive | Fluid movement |
> | Joyful | Internals in top shape |
> | Fabulous nails | Blood pressure O.K. |
> | | Terrific endurance |
>
> Attractive to my own eyes naked in the mirror
> Body doesn't move like concrete
> Body that supports the level of work/stress I am
>   up to
> Peace of mind knowing the energy is available

Use the blank box for your list.

Save this list for later reference. In step 5 these images of fitness results will be converted into specific, measurable goals.

STEP 2: TAKING RESPONSIBILITY FOR EXERCISE SLUMPS

Sometimes fitness results come slowly. The reflex habit of interested exercisers is to blame unfavorable circumstances for lack of results.

Maybe the health club has been infiltrated by singles who have migrated from the discos to the exercycles in quest of the perfect mate. Their come-ons are too great a distraction. Blame the singles!

The charismatic aerobics instructor with the Perfect 10 body has left for Hollywood and the search for stardom (or at least a role in an exercise video). She was the only one who could inspire you. How dare she leave! Blame the charismatic aerobics instructor!

The winter weather is no time to exercise. Who wants to jog through snowdrifts or bicycle on ice? Going out to the gym or swimming pool seems like so much effort on a cold dark morning or night. Blame the weather for your seasonal layoff!

The hit list never ends. There's always some person or circumstance to foul up your good intentions. While you wait for the situation to get better, your body steadily gets in worse shape.

Winston Churchill once said, "The price of greatness is responsibility." So is the price of fitness.

Taking responsibility for lack of results frees you from being a victim of circumstances. You stop waiting for the circumstances to change. You figure out what it's going to take to get your body in shape and go do it. Ultimately, it becomes clear that nothing is holding you back but the restrictions you impose on yourself. Taking responsibility gives you back the power of choice that you had unknowingly given away to circumstances.

MOTIVATION TRAINING SESSION: TAKING RESPONSIBILITY

Time: One or more ten-minute sessions.

Purpose: To break the habit of finding excuses to account for poor results. Recognize your own responsibility for your fitness. Plan strategies for overcoming difficulties in sustaining regular exercise.

If you were asked to explain why you're not in good shape, what would you say? If you're a regular exerciser, how come your vision for "a body that works" isn't reality right now? Go ahead and write down your reasons in the left column of the Commitment Balance Sheet. Be sure to include your Easy-Way-Out Traps. Go for quantity. A sample list of reasons might look like this:

I don't like pressuring myself to exercise.

The family needs me around in the evening.

There are unexpected meetings and deadlines.

It gets boring after about three weeks.

My workout partner is unreliable.

Finding parking near the gym is a hassle.

Now quickly review your list. Do you feel any differently about each item as a barrier to exercise, compared to the way you felt when you first started reading this book? Do you realize that by staying inactive you're letting these reasons replace the fitness benefits you really want? You're choosing to have reasons instead of results.

Review each reason again with the intention of disputing its power to control your choices. Ask yourself these questions:

Is this "difficulty" beyond my capacity to overcome? Is it just something I tell myself so I can avoid the effort it takes to be in shape?

Besides accepting this reason for not exercising, what other choices do I have? If the right conditions for exercising aren't in place, what can I do to create the right conditions?

What's it going to be—reasons or results?

With the exception of disabling injuries and physical limitations, most reasons—like those in this list—are simply your own perceptions of difficulty. Now go ahead and develop action steps to overcome such reasons for not exercising. Write your responses in the results column of the Commitment Balance Sheet. You might write down action steps like the following:

THE COMMITMENT
BALANCE SHEET

REASONS	DESIRED RESULTS

"There are lots of fitness activities that can be done with families such as walking, swimming, riding bikes. Great replacement for TV in the evening."

"Once I reach the office, I'm liable to be asked to stay late for a meeting or to solve a new problem. The only time guaranteed to be free is before work. So it's time to shift to morning workouts."

"Varying the form of exercise will keep it from getting boring. Besides, boredom is such a wimpy excuse. Once results start showing, it won't be boring."

"I must find a more reliable workout partner or just do it myself."

"I can ride my bike over to the gym and avoid parking hassles."

Review your Commitment Balance Sheet. So what's it going to be for you—reasons or results? *Choose.* Notice that when we're not committed, we choose reasons to replace the fitness results we really want.

Can you see the power that comes from refusing to accept excuses for exercise slumps? Recognize your responsibility for your physical condition. If you're in great shape, you're responsible. If you're in miserable shape, you're responsible. There's no hiding out from responsibility.

STEP 3: CREATING AN INSPIRING PURPOSE FOR YOUR FITNESS COMMITMENT

Your fitness commitment is very special. This is not a short-term project or campaign. There is no point of retirement from taking care of your health and fitness. Outside of marriage, where the commitment is "until death do us part," few commitments are lifelong. The thought of exercise being a lifelong endeavor can seem overwhelming. How do you develop such lasting motivation?

To do anything consistently week after week requires a compelling and inspiring purpose. This purpose must be a constant and powerful reminder of the value of being fit. It will cause people to stick with their workouts even when they have good reasons for slacking off. Before starting a fitness program, you must know *why* you're exercising. What's the win in it for you?

Most people have not developed a clear and motivating purpose for being fit. When asked, "Why do you exercise?" the classic response is some variation of "I want to look good, feel good, and be healthy." Unfortunately, these common reasons for exercising are unlikely to inspire lifelong exercise.

It's easier for most people to buy new clothes, put on jewelry and makeup, and get a tan to improve their looks, especially if they're not overweight. Eating favorite foods, drinking, going to the movies, being with friends, or taking a nap are fast and easy ways of feeling good. Most of us claim to be in satisfactory health simply because we haven't been ill or treated by a doctor recently. So why bother with exercise when there are easier ways to look good, feel good, and be healthy?

You may never have thought about your purpose in pursuing physical fitness. You may already have a purpose in mind but it doesn't seem to be working. In either case, creating a purpose that supports your fitness commitment is essential. It must have a wake-up effect like a splash of cold water on your face when you're sleepy. Once reminded of the value of being fit, you must be able to ignore the Easy-Way-Out Traps and go exercise.

If you lack a strong purpose for exercising, your choices are liable to be swayed by your momentary feelings, thoughts, and circumstances. Sometimes they will be conducive to exercise and sometimes they will discourage it. There is little possibility for consistency in your workout.

To be effective, your purpose must be expressed in a way that makes exercise an essential activity instead of being a daily choice that you have to think over. Exercise needs to fall in the same class as going to work or caring for your children. At times, you'd prefer not to work or to deal with your children, yet you do it anyway. It's almost as if you have no choice. The decision is automatic.

Your statement of purpose must:

1. be brief and easily memorized.
2. describe a purpose that is so important that reasons for taking the easy way out are insignificant by comparison.

3. be a constant reminder of why you go through the effort of exercising and staying in shape.

You need to condense your purpose into a fitness credo.

MOTIVATION TRAINING SESSION: FITNESS CREDO

Time: 45 minutes to an hour.

Purpose: To develop a brief statement of purpose or a fitness credo that supports your personal fitness commitment.

There are two ground rules for developing a fitness credo. First, **focus on the benefits, not the activity.** Lifting heavy weights can resemble self-inflicted pain unless you know why you're doing it. Running around a track makes no sense unless the benefits are important enough. Unless we can see value in an activity, we will stop doing it, especially if it seems difficult. It's necessary to discover: How does being fit contribute to your having what is important in your life? How does being fit contribute to realizing your personal definition of success?

Paradoxically, the difficulties that stop us from exercising can be used as motivators. The second ground rule is to **turn apparent difficulties into opportunities for breakthroughs.** Without commitment, your automatic response is to avoid difficulties. However, by approaching the difficulties and being successful, you immediately set up a breakthrough opportunity. Exercising in the face of bad circumstances is undeniable proof of your true capabilities. You're creating powerful evidence that the difficulties were all in your imagination.

Many of the obstacles that stop us in exercise also appear as barriers to results in other areas. What difference would it make in your life if you could eliminate the excuse "not enough time"? Imagine how much more productive you'd be if you could eliminate forever the image of "being a procrastinator"? If feeling bored is a frequent cause for your dropping out of jobs and relationships, how would your life change if boredom were eliminated as a viable excuse for quitting? Breakthroughs in a fitness program often cause ripple effects in relationships, work, and other activities.

In my work with many clients, I've discovered certain questions that guide people in clarifying the purpose of their fitness commitment. Write down your responses to the following series of questions.

Focus on fitness benefits,
not the activity
1. What exercise benefits do you find most appealing?

_____

_____

_____

_____

2. How would gaining these benefits improve your family life? Your productivity and satisfaction at work? Your social life or recreational activities?

_____

_____

_____

_____

3. What's missing from your life now? Would upgrading your physical fitness help you get part of what's missing?

_____

_____

_____

_____

4. Is there someone in your life like a parent, friend, child, business associate, fitness buff, or celebrity who has strengthened your interest in fitness? If so, what is it about your relationship with this person that motivates you toward accomplishing your desired fitness results?

_____

_____

_____

_____

5. Do you have a personal mission in life which can be facilitated by becoming more consistent with exercise, and growing more fit?

_____

_____

_____

_____

Turning perceived difficulties
into breakthrough opportunities

1. What is the primary barrier that keeps you from sustaining the fitness program you desire?

_____

_____

_____

_____

2. How does this barrier show up in other areas of your life to hinder your performance?

_____

_____

_____

_____

3. How is successfully sticking to an exercise program an opportunity to discard similar excuses that cause you to miss out on other things you want?

_____

_____

_____

_____

4. What new possibilities would open up in your life if you overcame the barriers that now stop you from exercising?

_____

_____

_____

_____

5. How will sticking with an exercise program and getting the results you want help get rid of a negative self-image (e.g., I'm lazy, I'm a quitter) and develop a more positive one (e.g., I'm energetic, I'm persistent)?

_____

_____

_____

_____

Developing Your Credo

Review your answers. Notice any patterns or insights. Remember that you are creating an inspiring purpose for your fitness commitment.

Consolidate your answers into a brief statement of purpose or credo. The credo should be no longer than seven words. It must be easy to memorize and repeat to yourself. Above all, it should represent, in condensed form, your purpose for exercising and being fit. It answers the question: *What is the purpose that would support your deciding to exercise during moments when you're tempted to miss or to cut down your program?*

The following examples contain important insights from my clients which led to creating their credos. Their credos are in italics.

- "Being overweight has caused me to hold myself back. I avoid speaking in large groups. When I go out dancing, I never let my body really move to the music. I'm awkward in meeting new people. I'm always feeling self-conscious. My whole life is spent trying not to be noticed. Losing excess weight is *my ticket to freedom.*"

- "My pattern is to start out projects with great enthusiasm only to have my interest drop and end up quitting. It happens with jobs, relationships, courses at college, diet, and exercise. I'm not sure

I can stick with anything. Staying on an exercise program will prove *I'm not a quitter.*"

- "I'm successful in my career, my marriage is terrific, and I love being a new father. My life is coming together except for my body. I used to be in great shape. Now whenever I look in the mirror, I'm reminded how far I've let myself go. I'm fed up with being dissatisfied with my physical condition. Getting back in shape eliminates the one area I know needs improvement. I'm ready to *go for completion.*"

- "My exercise program is similar to my work habits. I get off to a blazing start on projects, get exceptional results, and then start to coast. Same pattern for exercise. I do it faithfully and press myself for intense workouts for about a month and then return to a minimal maintenance program. Here's a chance to break the pattern and go for *sustained excellence instead of flashes of brilliance.*"

- "I've always been giving to my family and close friends but rarely take time for my own interests. Instead of seeing exercise as self-indulgence, I now see it as a way of keeping myself healthy and energetic so I can give more to my loved ones. So it's a matter of *get it to give it.*"

Do any of these statements sound like you? These credos were made by people who are now successful with their exercise programs. They have each discovered a purpose for exercising that is more powerful than any reason for avoiding it. Go ahead and write your credo in this box:

STEP 4: EXAMINING THE RISKS OF YOUR FITNESS COMMITMENT

One of my exercise clients described his insights into the risks of commitment with these words: "I always thought there were degrees of commitment. But it's really a black or white matter. Once you assume the no-matter-what posture, there is no turning back. It's risky to say you're going to exercise regularly when all your past history indicates you haven't been able to stick with it. Before when I thought I was committed, I would exercise so long as circumstances didn't get too difficult. I gave myself a safe way out. But true commitment means you take the plunge, handle problems, and follow through reliably. It's risky."

MOTIVATION TRAINING SESSION: FACING THE RISKS OF COMMITMENT

Time: One or more ten-minute periods

Purpose: To examine the risks involved in making your commitment to being fit.

The following questions are designed to uncover and resolve your risks in making a fitness commitment. Reflect on each question and concentrate on your immediate gut reactions. Don't bother writing. Just be ruthlessly honest in answering the questions to yourself.

- What are the risks in your committing to a regular exercise program?

- How much faith do you have in yourself to accomplish what you are setting out to do? If you're unsure, are you willing to make the commitment knowing there is no guarantee you'll succeed, only your word that says you'll do it?

- What do you fear it will mean about you if you commit to exercising and fail to do it consistently?

- How will you feel about yourself if you decide now not to commit to exercising regularly?

- What excites you the most about taking this risk?

- If you keep your promises to yourself regarding fitness, how will this affect your ability to keep other promises?

- Recall your purpose for being fit. What would it mean to achieve your purpose? Is it worth the risk?

- Are you willing to just accept your fears about this commitment in order to gain the benefits that could come with being a regular exerciser?

You've had the chance to examine the risks of your commitment. The greatest risk now is to forget about your past history with exercise and boldly declare your commitment. You didn't come this far only to fall back on your old reasons for not exercising. It all boils down to determining what you are committed to:

- Are you committed to avoiding the risks of failure or to getting and staying physically fit?
- Are you committed to avoiding difficulty or to being in shape?

It all seems so clear when commitment is the issue. Forget that your parents weren't fitness role models. Ignore your past inconsistency with exercise. Discard the fifty excuses you've used to explain exercise slumps. That's all camouflaging the real issue—your commitment.

Making a commitment is a courageous decision to do something no matter what. It is like an electric switch which has only two positions, on and off. When commitment is "on," the power is not electricity but self-motivation. Commitment is the make-or-break factor in producing results in fitness and in life.

STEP 5: SETTING GOALS AND MONITORING PROGRESS

Sherry is an "occasional exerciser." She swims or jogs whenever the occasion works out for her, usually once or twice a week. "I exercise to lose weight and because swimming is a relaxing time for myself away from family," she says. "Unfortunately, I'm gaining weight and feeling more stressed these days."

Sherry is making a key mistake. She's attempting an exercise program without setting specific goals. What is her desired weight loss? How much weekly exercise is needed to get sufficient relaxation and burn enough calories? What specific diet modifications must be included for weight loss? Having definite goals is very different from exercising when it's convenient.

Goal-setting paid off immediately for Sherry. She achieved her first goal of four thirty-minute swims each week. But Sherry didn't stop here. She decided to concentrate on speed in addition to endurance. Her new goal was to increase the number of laps and swim for forty-five minutes each time. Personal records were set week after week. Eventually, Sherry qualified for the masters swimming team. Without going on a crash diet, her weight loss exceeded the goal of two pounds per week. She lost over thirty pounds in the first two months.

In an uncanny way, Sherry's life circumstances were changing to accommodate her workout schedule. She met new friends who happened to be swimmers. Pool hours were extended to early morning, perfect for the summer when her children sleep late. Sherry's husband decided to go on a diet. Her low-fat meals were accepted by the whole family.

Goal-setting creates momentum for achievement. Results come rapidly. Once goals are accomplished, they are replaced by more ambitious ones. Confidence builds. Unfavorable circumstances seem to work out to support goal achievement. It all comes together.

The power of goal-setting shouldn't come as a surprise. Nearly every motivational program and success formula recommends goal setting. Nevertheless, most people fail to set goals, especially when it comes to their physical well-being.

Goal-setting is what makes exercise a planned activity rather than a spur-of-the-moment decision. Notice the difference between the questions "What do I feel like doing now?" and "What do I need to do to accomplish my goal?" Which question is more likely to lead to exercising? Without goals, most of us do what's easier, what's already a habit, or what feels comfortable.

Without goals as a constant reminder, we lose track of long-range results. Miss a workout and it never gets rescheduled. Gradually, three stomach routines a week become two, one, and then zero. Even consistent exercisers plateau and resist going for bigger goals. For months, you could be thinking about adding a Nautilus workout to go with your aerobics routine but the idea never goes any farther. The first step to take in advancing your fitness might be to commit to new goals in writing.

Why the resistance to goal-setting? What's the worst thing that could happen? You'll miss the goal. Is that so terrible? Missing goals is a signal to modify your exercise program or to adjust your time schedule. It's also a great time to reinforce your commitment. Notice what reasons you've used when falling short of goals. Discredit these reasons if they are not legitimate obstacles. Recall your fitness credo and your most desirable exercise benefits. Develop plans to handle troublesome situations where your follow-through on goals has broken down. As long as you are pursuing goals, success is possible.

Goal-setting is a system for turning your vision of "a body that works" into reality. Stick to your goals and the daily workouts will add up to your intended fitness results. A properly developed exercise program is filled with long-range goals, monthly goals, weekly goals, daily goals, and even workout performance goals (e.g., number of exercise repetitions, amount of weight lifted, number and speed of laps swum). Breaking down goals gives a sense of steady progress. Each goal achieved is a big reward that motivates us to keep up the effort. Gradually, we get closer to long-range goals. Goals which originally seemed so distant, maybe even impossible, become very tangible. Excitement grows.

MOTIVATION TRAINING SESSION: MONITORING PROGRESS TOWARD YOUR GOALS

Time: Ten minutes to set long-range goals. Ten minutes each week to set weekly and daily goals and to record results.

Purpose: To develop the habit of writing down specific fitness goals as part of a progress monitoring system.

The first part of step 5 is to determine your long-range goals. They should be challenging to pursue and satisfying to accomplish. Resist the urge to play it safe. Don't settle for goals that you'll reach automatically. Sustained motivation depends on a worthwhile payoff.

Refer back to your picture of "a body that works," done in step 1. The images and associations you wrote down have to be converted to measurable goals. For example:

Images and associations from step 1	Long-range goals
Terrific endurance	Run a complete 10K race
	Run at pace equivalent to "excellent range" on Kenneth Cooper's classic 12-minute run test of aerobic capacity (e.g., for women 30–39, 1.30–1.39 miles—see table in his book *The Aerobics Program for Total Well-Being*
Not skinny, not fat	Achieve body fat percentage below average for my sex
Attractive to my eyes in a mirror	Lose two inches around waist and one inch from thighs
Fitness that supports the level of work/stress I am up to	Do stretching, yoga, and an aerobic activity for one hour a day five days a week

In each example, vague images and associations are translated into specific goals. Effective goals are written down so you can tell whether they've been achieved or not.

Now that you have a feel for goal-setting, it's time to make entries on the Exercise Profile forms. Use the sample to draw up your form on an 8½" by 11" sheet of paper. These forms are designed to assist you in making goal-setting a habit and in managing your time for exercise.

A long-range goal might be set for a year in the future. Break down your long-range goals into smaller steps: three-month, weekly, and daily goals. This makes your long-range goals seem more achievable. For instance, if the long-range goal is to place in the top ten runners for your age group in a 10K race, a progression of goals might include the following:

- Jog a mile in 12 minutes.
- Run a mile in 8 minutes.
- Run 2 miles in 16 minutes.
- Do a 2-mile "fun run" (noncompetitive) in 14 minutes.
- Run 4 miles in 32 minutes.
- Run a competitive 10K race.
- For each future 10K race, decrease time goals to approximate what's needed to place in top ten for age group.

Select a form of exercise that will get the results you want and will be enjoyable. Different forms of exercise have different effects on the body. There

EXERCISE PROFILE FORM

Long-range fitness goals: _____

_____

Three-month fitness goals: _____

_____

_____

Week of _____

No–Matter–What Goals	Target Goals

Time of Day	Goal	Results	Comments
Mon.			
Tues.			

Time of Day	Goal	Results	Comments
Wed.			
Thurs.			
Fri.			
Sat.			
Sun.			

are four major factors to consider in putting together a balanced exercise program: aerobic effect, strength, coordination, and flexibility.

Aerobic exercises demand large quantities of oxygen for sustained movement and strengthen the lungs, heart, and other organs responsible for transporting the oxygen. To qualify as aerobic, the exercise form must meet three criteria. First, it must involve steady motion for a minimum of twenty minutes, without a pause. Second, it must be done vigorously, at sixty to eighty percent of the maximum heart rate for one's age group. Third, it must be done at least four times a week.

Aerobic exercises include running, brisk walking, jumping rope, cross country skiing, swimming, stationary cycling, rowing, and aerobic dancing. Besides being great for conditioning vital organs, aerobic exercises are the best for burning excess calories. Their greatest limitation is that they do very little for strengthening the muscles. Jogging does very little for flexibility; it can even increase rigidity and tension in the body. It's important to vary your aerobic exercises, especially for people over forty. It's also important to do proper stretching as a warm-up prior to an aerobic workout.

It would be nice if playing your favorite sport would give you all the necessary aerobic conditioning. Unfortunately, this rarely happens. Baseball, football, golf, softball, and volleyball require too much standing around to be aerobic. Heart and breathing rates are not raised to enough intensity or sustained long enough to get the conditioning effects. But if done vigorously for at least thirty minutes, downhill skiing, calisthenics, racquetball, tennis (singles), and brisk walking can qualify as aerobic.

Weight resistance exercise tones and builds muscle mass, but offers very little cardiovascular conditioning. It's possible to develop large muscles but have very poor cardiovascular fitness. This limitation can be overcome by following a circuit weight training program. The circuit consists of a five-to fifteen-minute warm-up, either riding a stationary bike or skipping rope, followed by nonstop movement through a sequence of weight machines.

Swimming is one of the most balanced exercises. Experts rate it as good in terms of flexibility, strength, and coordination. It is rated just a notch below running for aerobic benefits. The best thing about swimming is that it provides a full body workout. There are many fewer injuries in swimming than in running. The buoyancy of the water relieves excessive pressure on the joints and bones. A possible limitation of swimming is that it does not decrease body fat. In *Fit or Fat?*, Covert Bailey says that a swimmer's body conserves its fat to provide warmth and buoyancy during the exercise. Swimming is a solid aerobic conditioner, but you'd better add some other form of exercise if you're high in body fat.

If you're unsure of the exercises to do to meet your goals, seek out expertise. Read a book, attend classes, or consult with a fitness expert. If you are over thirty-five or are out of shape, consult with a physician before beginning your fitness program. Gathering this information is essential to proper goal-setting. The following publications are recommended for developing an exercise program:

Bailey, C. *Fit or Fat?* Boston: Houghton Mifflin Company, 1978.

Cooper, K.H. *The Aerobic Program for Total Well-Being.* New York: Bantam Books, 1982.

Hales, D., & Hales, R. E. *The U.S. Army Total Fitness Program.* New York: Ballantine Books, 1985.

Netter, P. *High-Tech Fitness.* New York: Workman Publishing, 1984.

Sorenson, J. *Aerobics Lifestyle Book.* New York: Poseidon Press, 1983.

Royal Canadian Air Force Exercise Plans for Physical Fitness. New York: Simon & Schuster, Inc., 1972.

President's Council on Physical Fitness and Sports. *An Introduction to Physical Fitness.* DSHS Publication No. (05)-8250068.

Editors of Esquire. *Esquire Ultimate Fitness.* New York: Esquire Press, 1984.

Weider, J. *Body Building: The Weider Approach.* Chicago: Contemporary Books, 1981.

Besides focusing on results, select a form of exercise you are likely to enjoy. If you favor competition, consider sports like tennis and racquetball. If music and dancing have appeal for you, aerobic dance might be perfect. Are you an outdoor person? Running and bicycling are marvelous ways to exercise while enjoying great scenery. There's a form of exercise to suit everyone's taste.

For each week, record "no-matter-what" and "target" goals. A no-matter-what goal describes what you are committed to doing without fail. There are no excuses (except major emergencies) for falling short of such goals. Target goals describe what you would like to achieve, but they are not firm promises. For example, the no-matter-what goal could be running one mile in twelve minutes at least three times a week. Your target goal might be running a mile in eleven minutes four times a week. Target goals should be a stretch to achieve.

Effective goals are stated in measurable terms. You should be able to tell whether you've matched the goals, exceeded them, or fallen short. Here are some measurable variables to use in exercise goal-setting:

- Time—number of workouts per week; number of consecutive minutes of exercise; speed in covering a distance.
- Repetitions of an exercise.

- Strength—number of pounds lifted.

- Changes in bodily proportions.

- Cardiovascular measures—heart rate.

- Distance covered (in jogging, biking, swimming, etc.).

Start gradually. Easy does it. If you're out of shape, don't exhaust yourself trying to make a whirlwind comeback. Quick-fix fitness is a great way to get yourself discouraged or even injured. Find out what you can do without overtaxing yourself.

To start in a running program, you might do a walk-run for twelve minutes. Measure how far you've gone in that time and you'll have a rough sense of your pace for a mile. Gradually build up to twenty minutes, then thirty minutes.

The old belief about running was that the more you run, the better the conditioning effect. In his latest research, Dr. Kenneth Cooper has found that running more than fifteen miles per week is more than is needed for basic conditioning. He recommends working up to two miles, three times a week at an eight- to ten-minute per mile pace as an aerobic minimum. The maximum is three miles at five times per week at the eight- to ten-minute pace. Running more than fifteen miles a week does little to improve conditioning. It just increases the chance of injury.

Beginning swimmers should start out lap swimming with their rest intervals matching their swimming time. That might involve swimming a lap and then resting for approximately the lap time. They should work first to a minimum of thirty minutes a day three days a week. Later, one hour a day five times a week will have terrific conditioning benefits.

In weight resistance training, the only way to gauge your starting weight is through experimenting. Select a weight which you can lift for at least eight repetitions but no more than ten to twelve repetitions. When ten to twelve repetitions are easy, select a heavier weight.

Write down your target and no-matter-what goals in the appropriate boxes on the Exercise Profile form on page 107.

The next step is to fill in the time-of-day and daily-goal columns. Make it a habit to plan out workout times **before** the week begins. Sunday night or Monday morning are excellent planning times. Schedule activity that matches your weekly target goal. Only by planning for the target will you have any chance to reach it. If your life is hectic and something always seems to come up, planning is essential for success.

As you get into the week, record results and comments each day. In the results box indicate whether you met, exceeded, or fell short of the goal. Be specific. In the comments column, write down your feelings and thoughts before, during, or just after exercising. This column is especially useful for studying your ability to be self-motivated. Write down any excuses you overcame in completing your workout. Sample entries might be:

"Thought about coasting through the run today. Once I got moving, I pressed hard and set a personal record. Felt fantastic."

"Almost skipped out on my stomach routine but did it anyway. Felt good to complete."

If you succumb to an Easy-Way-Out Trap, follow the same procedure. Write down the reasons you accepted for missing a workout, cutting it short, or giving it minimum effort. Staying conscious of the traps will help you to dispute them the next time.

Study the following example of a completed form.

EXERCISE PROFILE FORM

Long-range fitness goals: Run 10K race; lose 15 pounds; increase 5–10 pounds on all weight-training exercises.

Three-month fitness goals: Run three miles under 25 minutes; do 4 complete weight-training sessions; lose 6 pounds.

Week of March 15:

No–Matter–What Goals	Target Goals
3 one-hour weight-training sessions Run 3 miles in 27 minutes. Lose 1 pound.	4 one-hour weight-training sessions Run 3 miles under 26 minutes. Lose 2 pounds.

Time of Day	Goal	Results	Comments
Mon. 5:30 p.m.	1 hour weight training 3-mile run	Complete workout. Did it in 27.5 minutes.	
Tues. off			

Time of Day	Goal	Results	Comments
Wed. 5:30 p.m.	1 hour weight training	Did all exercises, except leg work.	Short on time.
Thurs. 7:00 a.m.	3-mile run	Did in 27 minutes.	Felt great to cut time.
Fri. 5:30 p.m.	1 hour weight training	Missed it.	Happy hour parties; bad time to schedule workout; rescheduled for Saturday.
Sat. 11:00 a.m.	1 hour weight training	Did it all.	Did extra hard workout.
Sun. 5:30 p.m.	3-mile run	Did it in 25.6 minutes.	Great finish for the week!

STEP 6: RECEIVING SUPPORT FROM YOUR MOTIVATIONAL COACH

In my corporate fitness projects, I have worked with hundreds of people who are struggling to be regular exercisers. In an opening seminar, participants learn to dispute excuses for not exercising and are guided through the commitment process. At the conclusion, participants are invited to pair up as fitness coaches. They support each other in sticking to their weekly exercise goals. After three months the entire group is assembled for a follow-up meeting. I always ask, "How many of you would have dropped out at some point if it hadn't been for your coach?" In most cases, at least 40 percent raise their hands.

Your coach's job is to increase your reliability in delivering on your weekly goals. The Easy-Way-Out Traps did not vanish when you declared your commitment. They will always be around tempting you to slack off your program. Sometimes the only reason you'll press yourself to complete a workout is the knowledge that you will have to report results to your coach. When we make promises to others, we are more reliable than when we keep our goals to ourselves.

What exactly does a coach do? Good coaches are both compassionate and tough-minded about results. They acknowledge effort, improvement, and results. At the same time, they refuse to accept excuses.

When you write down a no-matter-what goal, the coach takes this as a promise, not just something that looks good on paper. How willing would you be to receive support from a coach who refuses to tolerate excuses for missing workouts? Are you willing to receive that kind of no-nonsense, results-oriented coaching?

A coaching relationship will work only if you permit your coach to be unreasonable with excuses that jeopardize your weekly goals. Be aware that coaching is not nagging or pressuring. It is not someone forcing you to do something you don't want to do. You set your own goals. Your coach helps you to beat the Easy-Way-Out Traps and to stick to your goals.

Using a coach is not a sign of weakness. It is not an admission that you can't exercise by yourself. Instead, it proves your commitment is serious. World class athletes and high salaried professional superstars use coaches to bring out their best performance. They've been exercising since childhood. Their livelihood depends on keeping in shape. They get paid enormous salaries as a reward for superior physical performance. Nevertheless, they rely on coaches to get the competitive edge in training. If pros and peak performers can use coaching, why not you? A coaching relationship is a terrific opportunity to accelerate your fitness results.

MOTIVATION TRAINING SESSION: DEVELOPING A COACHING RELATIONSHIP

Time: Three five- or ten-minute sessions per week in meetings with your coach.
Purpose: To set up and hold fitness coaching meetings.

Who will be your coach? The coach doesn't need to be an expert in exercise physiology or motivational psychology. You don't have to be workout partners. But there is one basic requirement: Your coach must be committed to your success in getting fit. When excuses come up, your coach must keep raising the question: "What's it going to be, reasons or results?"

Your friends, co-workers, family members, fitness professionals, or a workout partner could all be good coaches. A coach is an enthusiastic cheerleader, a creative problem-solver, and an enforcer to keep you on line toward your goals. Choose someone who has these qualities and who cares about your physical well-being.

It takes courage to give someone the power to coach you. If you do choose to be coached, follow these ground rules for structuring your relationship. First, describe to your potential coach the nature of the relationship. This is especially important if you already have a personal or professional relationship. It's easy for the role of spouse, friend, boss, or co-worker to get blurred with the coaching relationship.

Tell your coach:

- your desired results, especially three-month goals.
- how you can best be supported to stick to your weekly goals.
- reasons you'll likely use when you fall short of no-matter-what goals.
- that he or she has your permission to dispute your excuses and get you back on the way to your exercise goals.

Say something like "I'm committed to losing ten pounds, completing the thirty-minute Nautilus circuit three times per week, and jogging thirty minutes four times each week for the next three months. I'd like you to support me in reaching these goals. I'd like us to meet three times a week so I can share my goals with you and report progress. My likely excuses are: not enough time, out-of-town travel, something came up at the last minute, and the cold weather. When you hear me using these or other excuses, challenge me to stick with my goals. Let's work out a strategy for getting me back to doing what I'd promised. I give you permission not to accept any excuses for missing workouts, except illness and injury. I will not consider you to be nagging, manipulating, or forcing me to do something I don't want to do."

Three brief meetings of about five or ten minutes per week should be adequate. The first meeting is for setting the week's goals. Check your calendar to troubleshoot any foreseeable difficulties (parties, travel, visiting in-laws, extra work). The second and third meetings are for progress checks. In progress checks, the coach's job is to praise successes, point out any Easy-Way-Out Traps, and plan corrective measures so missed workouts get rescheduled and completed. It's also useful to anticipate any problems and troubleshoot solutions. Difficulties such as vacation periods, weekend slumps, busy seasons at work, or out-of-town travel often require advance planning to insure completion of exercise goals.

Bring the Exercise Profile forms to coaching sessions. If face-to-face meetings are impossible, phone calls can work provided that the coach is mailed a profile form each week.

Here's an example of a progress check with Tom, one of my clients. Tom is a forty-six-year-old business owner from the Midwest. He's a former athlete who's been irregular with exercise for four years.

In reporting his results, Tom launches into a defense for having an off week: "My car was in the shop for repairs. My brother and I have been arguing over business matters. It's getting real tense between us. I've been depressed and worried. I think about exercise but can't bring myself to do it. Say something to motivate me."

"Sounds like you're giving a lot of significance to your circumstances," I replied. "You're using a streak of undesirable events to justify an exercise slump. You're demanding that your life be smooth sailing in order for you to stick with your routine. But Tom, can you expect your life to run smoothly all the time?"

"No way. It's unrealistic."

"So the only alternative is to keep your word about weekly goals, instead of using difficult circumstances as an excuse. Stop letting the circumstances dictate whether you exercise or not."

"But Art, these are really tough times. I'm sure they'll be over soon and I'll get back to my jogging."

"Tom, if I let you slide out now, I'm not doing my job as a coach. In the future, you'll just call the circumstances bad and you'll be off the hook with exercise."

"There I go again. Caving in to unpleasant circumstances. It's an old habit."

"Tom, this is a great breakthrough opportunity. Achieve your goals, even during a tough week, and you'll prove to yourself that you can be in control no matter what circumstances turn up."

In talking to your coach, take full responsibility for your successes and failures in reaching goals. Don't blame circumstances. Don't try to explain or justify what happened. If a goal is missed, examine how you kept yourself from reaching that goal. Plan corrective measures to get back on course.

Three brief meetings a week can make a huge

difference. Frequent meetings nip exercise slumps in the bud. These conversations will help you recognize solutions you were already aware of but hadn't gotten around to acting on. Making promises to your coach will be a reminder to stick with exercise when he or she isn't around.

You shouldn't think that having a coach is like being assigned to a probation officer. This is a very special relationship between two people sharing a commitment to results. Enjoy sharing your accomplishments with someone who cares about your fitness and health.

STEP 7: PREPARING FOR WEAK MOMENTS

It's not going to be smooth sailing just yet. The Easy-Way-Out Traps are a persistent and formidable mental habit. You've probably felt committed before, but the exercise spurt was only short-lived. So what can be done to stay motivated?

It's important to know how to combat the traps when:

- you're tempted to cut back or skip a planned workout.

- you're interested in intensifying your workout regimen but you keep procrastinating.

- you're considering dropping out of exercise or taking time off.

The proof of commitment is going ahead with exercise even when you're thinking about sloughing off.

The basic plan for sustaining motivation is simple. Whenever you begin to resist following through on your goals, practice these three steps:

STEP 1: RECOGNIZE THE EASY-WAY-OUT TRAP. Answer the question: "What am I telling myself that is discouraging me from exercising?"

STEP 2: DISPUTE THE TRAP. Ask yourself: "What are other possible perceptions of this situation that encourage exercise?" Anything to weaken the trap is useful. Recalling your credo is probably the most powerful dispute available.

STEP 3: TAKE ACTION. GO EXERCISE. The quickest and most enduring way to dispute a trap is by going ahead with your planned workout. Each time you do, reasons for not exercising lose legitimacy. Completing this step is a visible breakthrough.

Here's how five people followed these three steps to self-motivation.

EXAMPLE 1. John is feeling depressed because of work problems and troubles with his girlfriend. He's already skipped three workouts and is now seriously thinking about missing another. Here's how

John uses the motivation-building steps to return to his exercise program:

Step 1: Recognize the Easy-Way-Out Trap: "I'm telling myself that I'm feeling depressed so I can't possibly exercise."

Step 2: Dispute the trap: "Feeling depressed is not a reason for avoiding exercise. If I stop exercising I'll only create another problem to feel depressed about. I can exercise even when I'm feeling down."

OR

Recall your credo: "I'm in control all the way. Here's a chance to show I'm in control even when I'm feeling depressed."

Step 3: Take action: John goes ahead with his exercise. John's breakthrough is learning that he can exercise even when he doesn't feel like it.

EXAMPLE 2. Diana is a busy sales executive. She operates at a fast pace from the moment she reaches the office until closing time. For months she's intended to resume evening aerobics classes, but feeling worn out at day's end makes it seem impossible. Here's how Diana got herself motivated:

Step 1: Recognize the Easy-Way-Out Trap: "I've been telling myself that after a hard day's work all I want to do is go home and relax. I deserve to rest. I don't want to exercise after being under pressure at work for eight hours."

Step 2: Dispute the trap: "Instead of seeing exercise as more work, I can see it as the beginning of my break. Exercise revives my energy and makes me feel better. I can make the evenings more productive and fun."

Step 3: Take action: Diana goes for an evening aerobics class. What a pleasant surprise to feel energized by the class! After three weeks of this, her evenings at home don't look the same. Instead of napping in front of the TV set, she plays enthusiastically with her children. A new reserve of energy has now become available. Diana discovers that her fatigue is more a matter of expectation than of actual physical exhaustion.

EXAMPLE 3. Kathy used to peddle an exercycle for thirty minutes five days a week. She's taken a new job that requires longer hours. Her family complains about her not spending enough time with them. Sounds like a dilemma? Here's Kathy's solution:

Step 1: Recognize the Easy-Way-Out Trap: "I'm telling myself that I don't have time to exercise, that something always comes up to interfere with doing it."

Step 2: Dispute the trap: "Not finding the time means deciding to let my body get out of shape. My commitment means finding the time."

Step 3: Take action: Kathy calls a family meeting to explain the importance of her exercise program. She gains their support in clearing out time for her two weeknight workouts. Kathy will plan to have leftovers which her husband will reheat on at least one of the nights. Since the family loves oriental cooking, they can order it out another night. Everyone is happy when Kathy arrives home. Her energy and positive mood make the evenings delightful. In this arrangement, everybody wins.

EXAMPLE 4. Art has lifted weights five days a week for over a decade. New demands on his schedule (i.e., writing a book on exercise motivation) seem to justify cutting short the closing portion of his workout, the sit-ups and other stomach exercises. He has great reasons for excluding stomach work for "just this one night." Art maintains, "I'm already working out for an hour and a half. It's enough. I've got lots of other things to get done. Stomach work is boring."

Good reasons for bypassing the stomach. However, after a couple of months, Art's pants are getting noticeably tighter around the waist. That does it. He will have to find a time for daily abdominal work. But the only time is early morning. The idea of climbing out of bed, brushing his teeth, and exercising his stomach is not appealing. Art hates to even think of starting the day with sit-ups. Here's how Art overcomes his resistance to morning exercise:

Step 1: Recognize the Easy-Way-Out Trap: "I'm telling myself that I can't exercise in the morning. I'm a slow starter. I'm not a morning person."

Step 2: Dispute the trap: "Wait just a minute. How am I so sure that I can't exercise in the morning? It's only some idea I made up years ago. I've never tested it. If I'm going to keep my stomach flat, it's got to be morning workouts. The morning is the only time I can count on to exercise without feeling time pressures."

OR

Recall your credo: "My job is to *wake 'em up.* If I'm going to be credible in my mission to motivate other people to exercise, I've got to be able to motivate myself. My integrity is on the line here."

Step 3: Take action: Art finds he's very capable of exercising in the morning. In fact, stomach work before breakfast raises his energy for the start of a new day. The shower feels even better after working up a sweat.

EXAMPLE 5. The following coaching dialogue illustrates how three basic steps of self-motivation can develop in a conversation. During a recent exercise motivation seminar, Phyllis, a participant, said, "But Art, you've got to admit that jogging is boring."

I remarked, "Phyllis, are you willing to receive some coaching from me that will create a mind set that puts more pizzazz into you jogging?"

"Go ahead."

"Phyllis, have you ever gone jogging when it wasn't boring?"

"Of course, lots of times. I go through cycles when I'm fired up about it or when it's deadly boring."

"So you can feel fired up or bored while jogging. It's not something about the activity of jogging that automatically makes it boring. The source of your boredom is the images and words you concentrate on while jogging."

"That's a different way of looking at it. Makes sense."

"Recall one time when you felt fired up about jogging. Actually picture that run right now. Notice where you were and who was with you. What images and feelings come to mind?"

Phyllis closed her eyes, paused for a few seconds, and then slowly described this scene: "I am jogging along Puget Sound with my boss, Sandra. We are running stride for stride and breathing to the same rhythm. The sun is sparkling on the water. I love the feeling of warmth on my skin. I see the city skyline in one direction and the Olympic mountains in the other. The conversation is free and easy. There are no pretenses, no roles when you run. I'm concentrating on making efficient movements with my heels striking the ground and my arms swinging in a compact motion. Completing the run leaves me feeling confident. My energy is back after a long day. It's almost like taking an energy-boosting drug."

"Sounds terrific."

"I'd forgotten how wonderful jogging can be. If only all my runs could be like that one."

"The experience you just described is always available to you. It all depends on what you tell yourself. I'll bet that on days when it's boring you don't even notice the mountains, the sun, the heightened energy, or the rhythmic movement with your jogging partner. My point is that your experience of jogging is whatever you choose to concentrate on."

"So what you're saying is that I have a choice of concentrating on feeling winded, on soreness in my body, bad weather, or the repetitious movements—*or* on more positive associations. At any time, I can recreate positive associations to stay fired up."

"Exactly. Even when you feel bored with jogging you can still go ahead and do it anyway. Very often the boredom you imagined beforehand goes away once your body gets moving."

In each of these examples, the Easy-Way-Out Trap fades out and no longer controls the person's choice. Instead, the trap-disputing statement becomes the basis for making a choice to take action. This simple shift in what we tell ourselves makes all the difference.

In the beginning, you'll want to remind yourself to use these three motivation-building steps during weak moments. Be patient. Practice, practice, practice. These steps will become a habit. You will learn to master your own self-motivation.

The following table shows some common Easy-Way-Out Traps and suggests ways of disputing them. Read through the list. Locate your own excuses. Notice how they are disputed.

The Easy-Way-Out Traps	Disputing the Traps
"I'll feel self-conscious in an exercise class."	"I'm not doing it for them. I'm doing it for me."
"I've tried it before but never stuck with it."	"Because I quit before has nothing to do with what happens now. This is a brand-new opportunity."
"I just don't have enough willpower."	"Sticking with exercise is a great opportunity to improve my self-discipline."
"I'm not sure I'm motivated enough."	"Saying I'm not motivated enough is predicting failure before I even start."
	"The only way I can tell if I've got the motivation is by doing it. My actions are proof of my motivation."
"It's not the right time to start."	"I've been saying it's not the right time for months."
	"This is as good a time as any. My schedule will always be busy. There will always be problems to solve. Waiting for the perfect time means I'll never get started."
"It costs too much."	"I can't buy health once I've lost it."
	"It's costly not to exercise."

The Easy-Way-Out Traps	Disputing the Traps
	"There are lots of low-cost ways to get exercise."
"Something always comes up to stop me from exercising."	"I'm responsible for always letting something else take precedence over exercise. It's a choice on my part."
"I already drink, smoke, and eat too much."	"Start with exercise and chip away at the other unhealthy habits."
"I'm too far out of shape."	"Instead of accepting myself as being out of shape, I can start now to improve my fitness."
"Exercise is boring."	"It's inevitable I'll be bored at times. Who says I need to enjoy every moment or I shouldn't bother doing it?"
	"I could be looking for ways to make it more fun instead of complaining."
"Exercise reminds me of how out of shape I am."	"Maybe I need the reminder."
	Avoiding exercise has kept me out of shape."
"If I ever stop, I'll lose whatever I've gained. So why even start?"	"That's almost like saying 'Why live when I'm only going to die?'"
	"Who says I have to stop?"

The Easy-Way-Out Traps	Disputing the Traps
"It's too great a sacrifice."	"What's more important than my health and appearance? I can't afford not to exercise."
"I'm not sure exercise will work for me."	"The only thing I can be sure of is that if I don't do it, I'll get even more out of shape."
"I can't find the time."	"Make exercise a priority and time is available." "Not finding the time means deciding to let my body get out of shape."
"I'm on a diet. Exercising and dieting at the same time require too much self-discipline."	"The best weight loss results come from combining diet and exercise. Instead of just doing what's easier, go for the best results. That means diet and exercise."
"I'm in good enough shape without it."	"Not being overweight or sick does not mean I'm healthy."
"I don't want to exert myself more than I have to."	"Being careful of tiring myself limits my life."
"I'm too tired after a hard day's work."	"That's all the more reason to get more energy through regular exercise."
"I hate to plan and structure my life."	"Not scheduling workouts in advance hasn't worked. Time for a change."

The Easy-Way-Out Traps	Disputing the Traps
"I'm lazy."	"Calling myself lazy is an excuse. I can muster up the energy to do anything I want."
"I've missed five workouts. I'm a failure with exercise."	"Missing five workouts doesn't mean I'm a failure. I can start right up again tomorrow."

How does it feel to know that the traps that sabotage your fitness program can be discarded? There are many other ways to dispute the common Easy-Way-Out Traps. Have fun coming up with your own disputes.

MOTIVATION TRAINING: PREPARING FOR WEAK MOMENTS

Time: One or more ten-minute sessions.

Purpose: To practice disputing your Easy-Way-Out Traps for those weak moments.

Mastering self-motivation involves being prepared for the inevitable weak moments. Describe a scenario for a weak moment when you are tempted to take it easy instead of completing your exercise goals.

_____

_____

_____

_____

_____

_____

Fill in both columns of the following chart. In the left-hand column, write down the Easy-Way-Out Traps likely to appear in your mind. Complete the other column entries to reflect your choice and your action when you take the easy way out. The choice box is intended to spell out the choices you considered. Sample entries might be:

Do the full twenty-minute workout *or* cut it to ten minutes.

Go home and sleep *or* go straight to the health club for aerobics class.

Call my coach for support when my motivation is weak *or* wait until tomorrow's coaching session (and miss tonight's workout).

The action box is for reporting what you ended up doing.

In the right-hand column, write down what you will say to dispute the traps and what you will do to complete your workout goal.

Self-motivation requires reliability. Over and over again, what you say will be done actually happens. Your words match your actions.

Once you're clear about the Easy-Way-Out Traps, no excuse is acceptable. There's no hiding, glossing over, or

When I've taken the easy way out	When I stay committed to my exercise goals
Easy-Way-Out Traps:	**Disputes for Traps:**
Choice:	**Choice:**
Action:	**Action:**

rationalizing weak performance. You either participate in calisthenics or miss the workout. You swim for your goal of fifty laps or stop short at forty. You take a leisurely pace in your aerobics class or press yourself to "go for the burn." Strip away the reasons, and the results are all that count.

STEP 8: MAKING YOUR WORKOUT FUN

One of the primary reasons people quit exercising is because it becomes boring or isn't fun. Of course, basing your effort on feelings is falling into an Easy-Way-Out Trap. Nevertheless, why not consistently enjoy an activity you'll put many hours into over the course of a lifetime? Assuming you've selected a form of exercise you're likely to enjoy, here are some tips for making any workout routine fun and interesting.

Instead of using boredom as an excuse to quit, treat it as a signal to redesign your exercise routine. You can vary the form of exercise. Mix aerobic dance with jogging or swimming. Alternate working out with resistance machines and free weights. Find different places to hold your workouts. If you've been running on an indoor track, take to the outdoors and periodically adjust your jogging route. Pick up a health and fitness magazine each month and select new exercises to throw into your current program.

Get off to a positive start in each workout. Hold your own private psyching-up session before you even flex a muscle. You don't need an inspirational coach to get you motivated. Be your own cheerleader.

Concentrate on what you are saying to yourself that causes you to feel bored or to want to just go through the motions. Recognize such thoughts as the only thing holding you back from a terrific exercise session. It makes no sense to worry about tomorrow or to be frustrated with the past. Right now is all that counts. Start telling yourself inspiring things. Remind yourself of the benefits of being fit. Repeat your fitness credo. Recall your experience of a recent workout in which you gave your best. You'll be amazed at how a few minutes of mental adjustment gets you off to a good start. Before long, you'll complete the workout and forget how rotten you felt earlier.

It's extremely helpful to get an exercise partner who is both reliable and who is doing a comparable training routine. On days when you're tempted to miss a workout, you'll show up at the gym simply because you have an agreement with your partner. (In fact, I know two women who exchange their gym bags and workout clothes each day. If one doesn't show up, the other one can't work out.) And on days when you're inclined to give minimum effort, your intensity will often be increased by your partner's strong performance.

If you enjoy participating in group activities, an exercise class is the best situation for you. Most fitness instructors recognize the need to make exercise fun. The good ones project an infectious enthusiasm that grabs the entire group. Often people come into class feeling grumpy, but are quickly motivated by the high energy and cheerful mood of their classmates.

Music provides a motivating accompaniment to a workout. Develop your own customized audio cassette. Pick your favorite upbeat and inspiring tunes. Listen to your recording while commuting to your workout and while you're doing it.

The last thing to remember is that you are responsible for your experience of exercise. It's not the type of exercise that is boring. *You* make it boring or enjoyable. Once a fitness instructor was told, "You've got to admit that swimming laps is boring." He responded, "So you mean that being alone with yourself is boring." Enjoy the activity of exercise and the great results.

Breakthrough Lessons from Committed Exercisers

"Physical fitness is the basis for all other forms of excellence."

—John F. Kennedy

A breakthrough starts with a dramatic shift in how you perceive the circumstances in your life. It's as if blinders have been removed. Suddenly, long-standing barriers to performance don't appear so formidable. Comfortable choices are dismissed. Fear of the unknown is accepted. You're geared up to relentlessly go after a prized result. Procrastination, inconsistency, and plateaus are gone. Everything is clicking. Best of all, you get results beyond what you'd imagined were possible based on your past performance.

Breakthroughs appear to be caused by dramatic events. For instance, motivation to exercise often seems to depend on being shocked by the threat of declining health or by realizing you're grossly out of shape. Yet breakthroughs don't have to happen by chance. You can set out to have one. Instead of being a matter of coincidence, breakthroughs can occur by design.

For many people, putting together a lifestyle integrating physical fitness is a breakthrough. For them it may have seemed impossible to be a high achiever at work, have a satisfying family life, and still stay in good shape. After years of exercise start-ups, their physical fitness has continued to lag behind.

There are two choices available to them. One choice is to accept that exercise isn't going to fit into the overall plan. After all, there are just so many commitments one can make. Better to be satisfied with success with one's career and family. That's plenty. Besides, it's more comfortable to focus time and energy on areas yielding good results than to pressure yourself trying to fit in exercise.

The other choice is to go for a breakthrough. To go after having it all—success at work, strong family ties, and a fit body. Isn't a healthy, fit body going to support better results with family and work? The shift in perception that triggers a breakthrough happens when you see exercise not as an activity to do when time becomes available, but as something essential to achieving overall success.

This final chapter ties together a number of key principles for making such breakthroughs possible.

First, you will become aware of several widely accepted beliefs about habit change which are not only inaccurate but also make breakthroughs impossible. To counter these beliefs, you will be introduced to a set of "breakthrough lessons" which encourage prompt, easy, and dramatic surges in results.

When you're merely *interested* in being fit, your choices and actions will be influenced by customary "rules" of behavior change. These rules are not written up, distributed, and formally publicized. They are learned in subtle ways. In fact, you probably aren't even conscious of them. If asked to verbalize these rules, you couldn't do so. However, they control your behavior as if they were law. Unfortunately, adherence to these rules makes habit change very difficult.

There are five conventional rules of behavior change:

Rule 1: Changing a habit is difficult and takes a long time.

Rule 2: Past history accurately predicts future performance.

Rule 3: If life already seems busy, trying to do anything more means putting pressure on yourself.

Rule 4: You have to feel like doing something in order to do it.

Rule 5: Performance breakthroughs are the result of the right circumstances happening at the right time.

Upon first inspection, these rules probably make sense. You've been hearing them from other people for a long time. They seem to describe what actually happens in real life. You may even be wondering "Aren't they true?"

But while these rules reflect what's normal, they are not the truth and they do not reflect what's possible. The normal pattern is for habit change to be slow, filled with struggle and with lots of slips in performance. Lasting results are rare. Habit change is doomed from the start when success depends on "wanting it bad enough," "feeling up to doing it," or "having conducive circumstances in place."

Committed people have rewritten the rule book for behavior change. Operating under a different set of rules makes it possible for them to achieve breakthroughs. What are the rules followed by committed people? They've been mentioned in previous chapters. Now is the time to organize them so you can put them into practice.

Lesson 1: Habit change is quick and easy when commitment is present.

Consider some common habits like wearing seat belts, brushing your teeth, washing dishes, paying your monthly bills, and going to work. None of these activities require great intellectual or physical capabilities. It's the same way with exercise. With minimal training or instructions on technique, most people can walk, swim, ride a bike, or maneuver a rowing machine. Athletic prowess is not a prerequisite for exercising.

Why is developing the exercise habit a long, difficult, and unproductive activity for so many people? Clearly the barriers are mental, not physical. The greatest barrier to habit change is the habit of perceiving circumstances as difficulties. Once we shake the habit of seeing difficulty in exercise, and instead see the value in it, then habit change happens smoothly.

Take the habit of flossing your teeth. The first time your dentist prescribed flossing, you probably could think of a long list of difficulties: It makes a mess. It's hard to remember to do it. It takes too much time at night when you're eager to get to sleep or in the morning when you're rushed to get to work. Flossing is sometimes painful for the gums. When floss tears between the teeth, it takes extreme dexterity and patience to remove it. Besides, isn't regularly brushing your teeth good enough? As long as you pay attention to these hassles, flossing occurs sporadically.

But suppose your dentist communicates the importance of flossing, and you see value in it too. Wouldn't it seem ridiculous to let these minor inconveniences stop you? Once you floss regularly, the original list of difficulties seems amusing. Nothing more than weak excuses.

Developing the exercise habit is no different from developing the flossing habit. Perceptions of difficulty can be replaced with alternative perceptions that support your desired fitness results. Simply by going ahead and exercising you'll prove that the difficulty was nothing more than an illusion you made up.

Lesson 2: Current performance is determined by immediate choices and actions.

An infrequent exerciser once said to me, "I've been inconsistent with exercise all my life. I'm inconsistent now and I guess I'll always be that way. Art, can you help me?" Based on that statement there isn't any possibility of change for him. All the bases, past, present, and future, are covered.

The fatal error being made is using past history as a basis for predicting future performance. To some degree, we all do this. Instead of setting big goals, we get conservative and do what's reasonable based on past history. As an example, let's say you've played three hours of racquetball a week consistently for the past six months. You've thought about adding stretching or weight training to achieve a more balanced fitness program. However, you dismiss the idea as unrealistic. After all, three hours of exercise seems to be all you can afford.

Each of us has a past; how can we break free of it? But there is a major difference between "having a history" and "being your history." The pattern of going on and off exercise programs reflects only your choices and actions to this point. It is not a measure of your true capability.

Forget your past track record. Give yourself a fresh start. When you get to the point of exercising consistently, don't start wondering when it will end. Remember that past performance has no bearing on current performance unless you say it does. Break free of your past history. Even if you've been a life-long slug in regard to exercise, right now is the time to spring from lethargy, throw on your workout attire, and get your body moving.

Lesson 3: Time and energy are always available when we're truly committed.

At the prospect of doing one more thing, most people reflexively respond with "That will put too much pressure on me" or "I just don't have time." These responses are made without checking schedules or attempting to set aside the time for another activity. Is it any wonder that the most common reason given for not exercising is lack of time?

Have you ever noticed how time is suddenly freed up when we feel urgent about getting something done? Around April 15 every year, millions of Americans finally find the time to file income tax forms just before the penalty deadline. Notice how a salesman committed to winning the trip to Hawaii always has time to make an extra sales call, even late on Friday afternoon. Time is always available for the activities we are committed to doing.

It's also important to challenge the assumption that doing more adds stress and pressure to our lives. Our perceptions of time and productivity are again based on past history. We have a fixed sense of what can be accomplished in twenty-four hours, how much sleep we need, how long we should work each week. These standards are taken for granted. They are comfort zones. If exercise is perceived as being out of our comfort zone, then it is automatically resisted. No attempt is made to experiment with new ways of using time or increasing the pace of our daily activities.

Time problems cease once a commitment is made. During the grueling filming schedule for the movie *Rocky,* actor Sylvester Stallone said, "My life is so exciting, sleep is an intrusion." Accelerating the pace to achieve an important commitment is a new opportunity, not a burden or nuisance. Instead of feeling stress and pressure, we can feel excitement, pride, and satisfaction. What a wonderful feeling to lead a productive life in which all major commitments get accomplished!

Lesson 4: You can do anything you want regardless of how you are feeling.

It's one of those mornings when you're not feeling up to going for a scheduled jog. You tell yourself things like, "I'm feeling too tired. Shouldn't have stayed up to watch David Letterman. Besides, it's too dark out there. I'm not a morning person. My body isn't built to be exercised so early. It's so warm under the bedcovers. Another half hour of sleep will feel terrific. Enough with pressuring myself to exercise."

In this example, unpleasant feelings are the basis for a decision to miss the jog. Feeling tired and turned off by the prospect of a morning jog discourages exercise. Feeling attracted to extra rest and physical comfort prompts the decision to sleep in. The underlying premise for this decision is: "If you don't feel like doing something, then you shouldn't do it. If you feel like doing something you should do it."

We operate as if there is a direct link between

our feelings and our actions. Since feelings are fleeting, they are not a consistent source of motivation. Consistent exercise requires breaking this rule. Instead of basing decisions on "what feels good," we must base them on "what works" to produce desired results.

Lesson 5: *Life is a series of opportunities for breakthroughs.*

We spend so much of life gathering up "circumstantial evidence" on which to base decisions. When circumstances don't seem conducive to success, we avoid making a serious effort. It's only logical to wait for the right circumstances to be in place.

There's only one catch. The longer you put off effort, waiting for the right circumstances, the longer you put off getting results. What if your perception of favorable circumstances never materializes? How ironic—because *you made up* this image of the right circumstances! But by giving this image significance, you're undermining your own chances for success.

The right conditions are always in place just by your saying so. Ignore how the circumstances look. Boldly approach difficulties. Take action and demolish excuses. Suddenly, there are no difficulties that can stop you. *Presto,* like magic, the right circumstances have fallen in place. Your commitment produced a breakthrough.

GO FOR IT!

This time your experience with exercising is going to be different. It isn't a matter of "going on" or "trying out" an exercise program. This is the end of false starts. This time you are going the distance. Your commitment carries a conviction of "no matter what." It will be hard to go back to the Easy-Way-Out Traps and see them as anything but weak excuses. The exercise program that once looked like a struggle has now become part of a weekly routine.

The best payoff will be the fitness results you've worked so hard for. You'll be able to look back to the times when such results seemed impossible. At that moment, you will know firsthand the power of commitment.

You've probably come to realize that this book is really about more than just motivation for exercise. It is about breaking free of the habit of doing what's easier and calling it your best effort under the circumstances. It is about keeping commitments to results no matter what difficulties get in the way.

Getting physically fit is only a small piece of what's possible for you as a result of sticking to your exercise program. Making the transition from irregular to consistent exerciser proves you've got what it takes to meet difficulty head-on and to carry through on a commitment. Your success in the physical arena can be extended to other parts of your life.

Neitzsche wrote:

> "If one will attempt the most difficult endeavor his mind can possibly conceive and is successful in that venture, then for the rest of his life, everything else will seem easy by comparison."

Knowing how to sustain a commitment to physical fitness can have ripple effects in every area of your life. Committed action turns imagined possibilities into tangible results.

GO FOR IT—FULL BLAST!

EXERCISE PROFILE FORM

Long-range fitness goals: _____

_____

Three-month fitness goals: _____

_____

_____

Week of _____

No–Matter–What Goals	Target Goals

Time of Day	Goal	Results	Comments
Mon.			
Tues.			

Time of Day	Goal	Results	Comments
Wed.			
Thurs.			
Fri.			
Sat.			
Sun.			

EXERCISE PROFILE FORM

Long-range fitness goals: _____

_____

Three-month fitness goals: _____

_____

_____

Week of _____

No–Matter–What Goals	**Target Goals**

Time of Day	Goal	Results	Comments
Mon.			
Tues.			

Time of Day	Goal	Results	Comments
Wed.			
Thurs.			
Fri.			
Sat.			
Sun.			

EXERCISE PROFILE FORM

Long-range fitness goals: _____

_____

Three-month fitness goals: _____

_____

_____

Week of _____

No–Matter–What Goals	Target Goals

Time of Day	Goal	Results	Comments
Mon.			
Tues.			

Time of Day	Goal	Results	Comments
Wed.			
Thurs.			
Fri.			
Sat.			
Sun.			

EXERCISE PROFILE FORM

Long-range fitness goals: _____

_____

Three-month fitness goals: _____

_____

_____

Week of _____

No–Matter–What Goals	Target Goals

Time of Day	Goal	Results	Comments
Mon.			
Tues.			

Time of Day	Goal	Results	Comments
Wed.			
Thurs.			
Fri.			
Sat.			
Sun.			

EXERCISE PROFILE FORM

Long-range fitness goals: _____

_____

Three-month fitness goals: _____

_____

_____

Week of _____

No–Matter–What Goals	Target Goals

Time of Day	Goal	Results	Comments
Mon.			
Tues.			

Time of Day	Goal	Results	Comments
Wed.			
Thurs.			
Fri.			
Sat.			
Sun.